BIOLOGICAL
PSYCHOLOGY
THIRD EDITION

CONNOR WHITELEY

ACKNOWLEDGMENTS

Thank you to all my readers without you I couldn't do what I love.

INTRODUCTION

How does our biology affect our behaviour?

That is the question biological psychology aims to answer from the role of the brain and its many brain areas to the role of neurochemicals to the role of sleep. This book will be exploring a very wide range of topic to answer this question.

But I've heard from a lot of people that our biology doesn't affect our behaviour. This couldn't be further from the truth because if it was a lie then I wouldn't be able to write 25,000+ words on the topic.

Also, I've heard people say this isn't proper psychology, and psychologists study the mind.

Again, this is another understandable misguidance because psychology studies behaviour and if our biology affects our behaviour then psychology will study it.

Why This Book?

I know what you're thinking, this is just another biological psychology book and it is, but it isn't.

If you want a long boring textbook to explain biological psychology to you, please don't buy this book.

Instead, if you want to an engaging, easy to understand book on biological psychology that will explain the field in-depth, but in an easy-to-understand way. Then please buy this book.

Plus, this book is on its third edition so that's plenty of great content for you to enjoy.

Whether you're a high school or university student, a trained psychologist or someone else interested in psychology. Then you should certainly get something out of this book.

Who Am I?

If you've read any of my other books, then you know I always like to include this section because I like to know who's talking to me when I buy a book.

So, in case you're like me, I'm Connor Whiteley, an author of over 30 books and 12 of these books are psychology books. Ranging in topics from biological to social to clinical psychology.

Also, I'm a university student at the University of Kent studying Psychology with Clinical Psychology and a Placement Year.

Finally, I'm the host of The Psychology World Podcast available on all major podcast apps. Where I talk about psychology news and different psychology topics each week.

So now the introduction is done, let's start learning about the great topic of biological psychology.

PART ONE: INTRODUCTION TO BIOLOGICAL PSYCHOLOGY

CHAPTER 1: HISTORY OF PSYCHOLOGY

Before we can learn about the present knowledge in psychology, we must first learn about the past.

Whilst, it's very hard to pinpoint the start of psychology. We know that interest in human behaviour started around 400 BCE when Plato decided to use the term Psyche to describe the mind and soul.

<u>Pre-Psychology:</u>

Before the field of psychology was founded, we had natural philosophy. That started to enquire about behaviour and other matters and there were multiple influential thinkers that debated behaviour.

For example, Plato believed that our nature, so our biology determined our behaviour.

Whereas Aristotle believed that nurture or the

environment caused our behaviour.

In modern terms, we call this the Nature-Nurture Debate but it does need to be updated as biological and environmental factors work together to form a behaviour.

The clearest examples of these factors working together can be found in Abnormal Psychology and the Psychology of Relationships.

Another notable figure in philosophy is Descartes in the 17th century who prosed the idea of the mind-body dualism.

In short, he thought that the mind and body were two separate entities.

Finally, you have Franz Gall (1758-1828) who believed that the brain and mind are linked by size and this idea later developed into phrenology.

However, this 'field of science' was far from scientific as there was no proper testing as well as it was largely based on anecdotal evidence. Which can be flawed.

Birth of Psychology

After Natural Philosophy, in the 19th Century psychology was born as Helmholtz started to research reaction time and physiological responses as well as Wundt set up the first psychology lab.

Wundt and Structuralism:

Although, during the birth of psychology, there were a lot of opposing viewpoints; like there is in psychology today; and one of these viewpoints was structuralism.

This was proposed by Wundt and it focused on the structure of psychological processes as well as it used introspection as people did tasks to gather data.

Nonetheless, introspection isn't the best method in testing as it can be inaccurate as people can be wrong as we can't always predict our own feelings.

Functionalism:

Subsequently, in opposition to Wundt's Structuralism, James came up with Functionalism that focused on the function of psychological processes in our lives, Darwinian theory and evolutionary fitness.

In other words, how the behaviour evolved over time to aid in our survival and function in our lives.

CHAPTER 2: LOCALISATION

The first stop on our journey to understand how biology can affect our behaviour is the theory of localisation.

Localisation is the theory that certain areas of the brain are responsible for certain psychological functions.

A possibly simpler way to think about it is that certain areas of a computer are responsible for its functions.

For example a hard drive stores information much the same way how the brain stores memories.

Furthermore, there are two types of localisation:

- Strict localisation which in its simplest terms means that one area of the brain is responsible for a psychological function.

- Weak localisation which is the idea that one area of the brain is dominant in a function, but other areas of the brain may take over its function as well.

In addition, some support for localisation can be found in these speech conditions below.

<u>Broca's Aphasia:</u>

We're going to look at this condition in a case study in a moment but this condition results in a serious impairment in language production. Resulting in the person with the condition omitting most pronouns, predisposition, conjunctions, auxiliary verbs, tenses, number and endings during speech production.

Although, their language comprehension is usually good, but there can still be deficits in this area when the sentence structure is complex.

Also, people with Broca's Aphasia have difficulty understanding the same kinds of words they omit. Like: prepositions and conjunctions.

Thankfully, they are aware of their condition and respond to therapy.

Overall, this shows the Broca's areas seems to be critical for understanding some, but not all, aspects of grammar.

Wernicke's Aphasia:

Another noteworthy condition is Wernicke's Aphasia which is caused by damage to the Wernicke area. This results in impaired language comprehension and impaired ability to remember the names of objects.

Interestingly, this is sometimes called 'fluent aphasia' because the person can still speak smoothly.

Thus, their grammar is not impaired but their speech lacks meaning and cohesion as well as recognition of items is not impaired but their ability to find words is.

Typical Characteristics:

- Articulate speech/ fluent speech except with pauses to find the right words.
- Difficulty finding the right words, anomia refers to the difficulty to recall objects.
- Poor language comprehension- difficulty understanding spoken and written speech (especially nouns and verbs)
- Lack of self-awareness- frustration and unresponsive to therapy.

Research into this area started over 150 years ago with our first case study.

Paul Broca (1861)

Broca was a French physician who treated a man for gangrene fever called: Lebrogne. By the age of 30, Lebrogne had lost the ability to speak and communicate.

However, all of his other functions were still in tac as when you tried to talk to him, he understood and tried to communicate back. Nevertheless, he could only say the word 'Tan' which he usually repeated twice.

His condition was named: Broca's aphasias- the loss of articulated speech.

When 'Tan' died aged 50 a brain autopsy discovered a lesion in his frontal left hemisphere of the brain.

If you wanted to be specific... it was in the posterior inferior frontal gyrus area.

Now that's a mouthful!

After this discovery, Broca named the area of the brain after himself and concluded after studying another 25 patients that the Broca area was responsible for the forming of articulated speech.

Overall, this study supports the idea of strict localisation because it shows that if the Broca area is damaged that the function of speech is impaired as well.

Critical Thinking:

One aspect of the study that makes it good is that Broca studied another 25 people before drawing his conclusion. Meaning that he had a large sample size so his conclusion could be supported.

However, Broca preserved Tan's brain and 100 years later it was dissected, and the researchers found that the lesion wasn't as neat nor confined to the Broca area as previously thought.

So, it is possible that the Broca area isn't responsible for speech?

It is possible that another area of the brain that was affected by this lesion was, in fact, responsible for the forming of speech.

Further support for localisation:

Each of these lobes plays a key role in behaviour:

- The Frontal Lobe- associated with executive functions. Like planning, decision making and speech.
- The Occipital Lobe- associated with sight.
- The Parietal Lobe- associated with the perception of stimuli.

- The Temporal Lobe- associated with hearing and memory.[1]

Also, certain hemispheres of the brain are more dominant over certain functions. For instance:

Left Hemisphere Dominance:

- Visual, auditory, language
- Speech
- Verbal memory
- Analytic, sequential/temporal processing

Right Hemisphere:

- Tactical patterns
- Nonverbal memory
- Spatial functions
- Recognition of music, emotions and faces.
- Holistic, spatial/ parrel processing

Lashley (1929)

On the other hand, not all functions of the brain are localised. One example that we'll look at now is memory.

In a typical experiment, he would train a rat to go through a maze to find a food pellet without an error.

---

[1]

https://www.thinkib.net/psychology/page/22420/localization
-plasticity

Following this, he would remove a part of the brain. These removed sections would range from 10% to 50%.

The point of removing certain areas of the brain was that if the memory was stored in one place then if you removed certain areas of the brain one at a time you would eventually find it.

The results of his experiment didn't support his theory that memory was localised. Therefore, he decided that it was because the amount of brain matter destroyed impacted memory and not the location. (known as the principle of mass action) and because one area of the brain could take over the function of another area of the brain. This is known as equipotentiality.

Therefore, as Lashley couldn't find an area of the brain responsible for memory. This doesn't support the theory of localisation, and he proposed that memory is evenly spread out through the brain.

His theory is generally accepted today but memory is known not to be as uniformly and evenly spread out as Lashley thought.

Critically Thinking:

While Lashley did manage to prove that memory is not localised to one area of the brain. It begs the question and opens up the classic psychological debate of how far can we compare animals to humans as while we share a lot of our DNA with rats. As a result of physical differences and differences in our brain. Can this conclusion be accurately applied to humans?

Conclusion:

Personally, I think that we can agree that certain areas of the brain are localised to specific areas. While others are not.

What do you think?

Overall, localisation can affect behaviour because it demonstrates that certain areas of the brain are responsible for key behaviours that are important to humans. For example, the Broca area is responsible for articulated speech which is important for the survival of the species. The ability to communicate with one another.

CHAPTER 3: NEUROPLASTICITY

This really has to be one of my favourite parts of biological psychology because I found it so amazing that our brains can change relatively quickly in response to our needs.

Neuroplasticity is the ability for the brain to change itself in response to what the environment demands of it.

This process happens because our brains make and break the connections between our neurons; think of neurons as the wires in a computer connecting all the parts of the brain together; so that our neurons can be remade to form new connections.

Development of The Brain:

However, if we want to understand how neuroplasticity works, we need to understand how the brain develops.

Therefore, the development of neurons in the brain involves four processes.

Firstly, new cells are produced via cell division and this is called meiosis and mitosis. As well as the cells reach their target destination by the process of migration.

Next, the cells specialize and form their unique axons and dendrites. This is known as differentiation.

Subsequently, through the process of myelination, the glia cells (we'll look at this later) produce a myelin sheath around the axon to accelerate transmission.

Finally, the new cells go through synaptogenesis. This is the formation of new synapses.

If some of that has gone over your head or if something isn't clear. It will all be explained in the nervous system part of the book.

Neural Competition:

Since neuroplasticity is about the brain forming new connections, it begs the question: what causes a neuron to die?

Despite there being several factors that determine this, Nerve growth factors (NGD) are a type of neurotransmitter released by muscles that promote the survival and growth of axons.

Thus, without these Growth Factors, the neuron dies.

This enables the exact matching of the number of incoming axons to the number of receiving cells.

Since it would be very ineffective of the body to have hundreds of axons releasing neurotransmitters without there being another neuron nearby to deal with the information the releasing neuron is trying to communicate.

After maturity, the apotheosis (or killing) mechanisms become dormant.

Myth Busting:

Personally, I love myth-busting because there's a lot of false facts in popular culture about the body so you will see a few sections dedicated to busting myths.

For example, there's no truth to the myth your brain and eyes don't grow once you're born.

Due to a 1-year-old's brain is 185% bigger than it was at birth as well as an adult's brain is 20% to 30% bigger than it was at the age of 1.

Fine-tuning

If you've done child development or read my book Developmental Psychology, then you'll know the brain needs to fine-tune itself to increase efficiency.

Consequently, the brain has a limited ability to reorganize itself in response to experience. As well as the loss and gains of spines on the dendrites indicate new connections and potentially new information processing.

Interestingly, according to Sadato et al (1996, 1998) people who have been blind since they were born, experience brain reorganisation, also known as neuroplasticity. With, the primary and secondary visual cortical areas activating during tactile tasks. Showing how the tactile regions of the brain had used the unused visual cortex.

This will become clearer in a study below.

Language Learning:

Personally, I love language despite my own speech problems and language is a great example of how the brain changes.

Since there's a critical period for learning language skills and if you don't learn it during this period. Then you may never learn these skills. (Lenneberg, 1967)

Also, learning a second language differs as a function of age, because early exposure to some language increases the ability to learn another language later.

Additionally, Mechelli et al (2004) was the first study to suggest changes in the GM as a result of bilingualism. As well as newer studies have shown sustained similar effects in language areas. (Stein et al, 2012, Crogan et al 2012, Pliastsika et al 2014)

Also, increasing evidence offer effects on the structure of working memory tracts that connects language areas. (Luk et al, 2011; Mohades et al, 2012: Pitatsikas et al 2014)

Overall, these studies show the effects of language has on the brain and how the brain needs to change due to language demands. For example, the working memory tracts in the brain changes to connect to more language areas.

Merzenich et al (1984)

Personally, I do like this study because the first time I read it. I was surprised to find out the results; which you'll see in a minute; as I never expected the brain to be able to change to that extent.

Moving onto the study, the researchers got 8 adult owl monkeys and attached electrodes to their head and then stimulated each finger of the hand. In order to map the areas of the brain responsible for each finger (digit).

The results of this mapping showed five distinct areas of the brain.

Afterwards, the researcher chopped off the third finger of each monkey.

After 62 days, another mapping was done, and results showed that the areas of the brain responsible for the first and fifth digit had stayed the same.

However, the areas responsible for the second and fourth digits are expanded into the now unused space where the third digit was located.

In conclusion, it takes 62 days for the brain of an Owl monkey to remap itself in response to injury.

This study is linked to neuroplasticity because it demonstrates how the brain can remap itself to respond to the environment. In this case, the injury.

Critical Thinking:

This study shows how the brain can change itself in response to injury. Which is what the study was meant to be measuring. (this is known as internal validity- measuring what was intended to be measured)

However, by the 62-day mark, the remapping was complete. So, did it take 62 days to remap or did it take 36 days to remap? As a result of this, we cannot say with any true accuracy how long it takes for a brain to remap itself.

Another study that demonstrates the interesting effects of neuroplasticity is:

Draganski et al (2004)

The research took people and divided them into two groups: the jugglers and the non-jugglers. No one had any prior juggling experience.

Everyone had a brain scan at the same time during the experiment.

Firstly, everyone had a brain scan then the jugglers practised a basic juggling routine for 3 months. This was followed by another brain scan.

Finally, the jugglers didn't practice their routine for 3 months followed by a final brain scan.

The results have shown for the first scan, there were no differences in the structure of the two group's brains.

However, for the second scan showed increased brain matter in certain areas of the brain; like the temporal lobe; for the jugglers.

For the third scan, these areas of the juggler's brain had shrunk but not to their original size.

In conclusion, brain matter increases in response

to learning; the environment; but if this new skill isn't practised or needed anymore then this brain matter decreases but not as much as before though.

Overall, this study supports the idea of neuroplasticity as it shows the brain changes in response to learning.

Critical Thinking:

The study was well controlled because it made sure that no one had any prior juggling experience so everyone would be in the same situation and their brain structure would be the same.

Although, the study has low ecological validity; meaning you can't generalise the findings in the real world; because not a lot of people juggle in the real world, but could the results be applied to a more everyday task? Such as cooking, washing or tying shoelaces. Unless research is done into this we might never know.

Conclusion:

On the whole, neuroplasticity affects behaviour as it allows the brain to remap itself appropriately so that we can maximise how good we are at a given skill.

For example, Draganski (2004) shown us that the brain changes in response to learning so it's possible and equally possibly a stretch but this could allow our brains to develop so we can be better at our jobs and our hobbies.

Both increases our chances of survival from a monetary point of view but equally increases the pleasure we get from doing our hobbies and interests well.

It's just an idea.

It's this chapter and the chapter before why I find psychology and biological psychology interesting, because I feel that we don't give our bodies enough credit sometimes. Or we simply don't recognise how important our bodies are in relation to how we behave.

CHAPTER 4: NEUROPLASTICITY BY BRAIN DAMAGE AND LATERALIZATION OF FUNCTION

So far, we've looked at neuroplasticity that's caused by environmental demands but the brain can remap itself as a result of brain damage as well.

For example, some possible causes of brain damage are:

- Stroke, tumours and infection,

- Exposure to toxic substances.

- Closed head injuries

- Degenerative diseases.

Diaschisis:

Building upon this fact, following brain damage, the surviving brain areas tend to increase or reorganise their activity.

Due to activity in one area stimulates other areas but damage to the brain disrupts these patterns of normal stimulation.

Resulting in the brain having to reorganise itself to try and react to this normal pattern of stimulation.

One way to aid recovery is the use of drugs to stimulate activity in the healthy brain regions after a while might be a mechanism of later recovery.

Reorganised and Sensory Representations:

You might be familiar with the cortical homunculus and this is a representation of what the human body would look like if our body parts were the same size of the area of the brain dedicated to their sensory details.

For example, our hands and genitals would be a lot bigger than our back as these body parts are more sensitive and they take up more room in the cortical area of the brain.

This is related to neuroplasticity because these brain areas can reorganise themselves. As seen in Merzenich et al (1984)

Lateralization of Function:

This leads us into our next topic about lateralization since the brain is separated into two hemispheres. As well as the information that comes into our right eye is processed by the left hemisphere of our brain.

This is interesting because the corpus callosum joins these two hemispheres together and to stop severe epilepsy. This needs to be cut.

Resulting, in several interesting effects. For instance, when information comes into the right eye and it's processed by the left hemisphere.

However, as the corpus callosum is cut they are unable to say the name of the object, but they can draw it.

Nonetheless, in terms of research, using split-brain patients is not ideal because these people already had abnormal brains before the operation and the operation can vary since each operation differs in how much of the corpus callosum is cut.

This makes it difficult to treat the group as uniform.

Furthermore, this a small sample of participants and not all epilepsy patients undergo callosotomy.

Lateralization of Emotion Processing:

Another example of lateralisation is that emotional processing is a function of the right hemisphere as supported by Carmon and Nachslon (1973).

A Cautionary Note:

Similar to the limitations of localisation, I must add that lateralization of function is the exception rather than the rule, as well as laterality, is relative and not absolute.

Also, the research surrounding lateralisation could be argued to be bias because most of our knowledge of brain mechanisms comes from the study of people with brain damage.

So, without more research on people with 'healthy' brains, the results aren't absolute.

Furthermore, the left and right dominance of function is affected by gender and handedness, because 90% of humans are right-handed and 10% are left-handed.

All these individual differences that make us unique and great, impact our brain.

CHAPTER 5: GENETICS

This is one of the most historical and classical arguments. What out of biological or environmental factors are the primary force responsible for behaviour?

Although, since behaviour is the interaction between genetics and the environment, the more modern version of the argument is essentially focusing on how the factors of the two interact with one another to create a behaviour.

The easiest example of this is with depression because as I'll tell you in a minute it has a genetic base but to what extent does the environment impact on it as well?

Since surely loss of family, thinking style and other factors affect the development of depression as well.

What is a Gene and DNA?

Before we jump into the studies showing that genetics affect behaviour: what is a gene?

A gene is a part of your DNA responsible for a specific trait or behaviour.

Moreover, DNA is a double-stranded molecule containing genetic instructions. Allowing the body to replicate that piece of DNA. Which is made up of 4 chemicals. These are: Adenine, Guanine, Cytosine and Thymine.

With each base (the link of these chemicals) being made up of one phosphate molecule and one sugar molecule.

Overall, these chemicals link together to form DNA and the genetic instructions. They link together as:

- a-t

- g-c

Building upon this further, there is about 3 unique bases to human DNA and the order of DNA is very important. Due to the body reads DNA like chunks of words and each locus on a strand of DNA means something to the body. The specific locus is called a gene.

This is the process of making an RNA copy of DNA as well as this means more DNA for new cells can be produced, and it happens in the following way.

Firstly, the DNA helix unwinds and the process begins when the RNA polymerase enzyme starts RNA synthesis, and this continues for 1 whole gene.

Afterwards, the new RNA strand separates from the DNA and then the RNA strand is used as a template to make new proteins.

Strange Genetic Facts:

To highlight the point above about the order of DNA is very important, I want to mention these facts to you:

- You share 99% of your DNA with me.

- You share 98.7% of your DNA with a chimpanzee.

- You share 50% of your DNA with a banana.

In other words, if your DNA was reordered you might turn into a Chimpanzee or worse a banana!

So, let's start seeing how our genetic makeup affects our behaviour.

Caspi et al (2003)

In this study, you'll hear about a word called alleles. This is a version of a gene.

A Longitudinal study; a study over time; of 1,037 children from New Zealand was divided into three groups: people with two short alleles of the 5-HTT gene, one long and short alleles, two long alleles.

They were assessed from the age of 3 to 25.

A life history calendar was used to assess stressful life events.

Subjects were assessed for depression with an interview and information from someone who knew them well.

Results showed that there were no differences in the number of stressful life events but people with two short alleles managed life events with more depressive symptoms.

Critically thinking:

The study effectively looks at the genetic argument for depression.

Nonetheless, this study does have ethical concerns. For example, the distress that knowing that you're genetically more likely to develop depression can cause.

Therefore, the costs and benefits of research

must always be calculated before research is done.

Bouchard et al. (1990)

It was a longitudinal study with over 100 sets of identical and non-identical twins that were raised together and apart all over the world.

The researchers gave them over 50 hours of psychological and physiological testing.

The results showed that the similarity rates between identical twins that were raised apart were approximately 76%. Then Bouchard determined a heritability estimate of 70% of intelligence attributed to genetics, and 30% to other factors.

Critically thinking:

The results of the study have been supported by other studies making its results more credible.

But the study assumes that twins that were raised together experienced the same environment. Therefore, a question to you as the reader is: did you experience the same environment as your brother or sister? Even if you weren't twins, I think the answer still applies.

Twin Studies Sources of Error:

Whilst we're on the topic of twin studies, there are several places where error can be introduced.

For instance, in fraternal twins, their interaction with the environment increases the variance in the study.

The differences in the prenatal environment is linked to this criticism. For example, smoking and the stress the mother experiences.

Another source of error is how people treat genetic twin and fraternal twins differently.

A lot of studies use twins that have been separated by adoption and foster care and thankfully these children are placed in low-risk families.

Therefore, this introduces a difference in the risk each twin is exposed to.

Finally, the relatively low frequency of adoption limits the research sample.

This causes additional problems with the generalisability of the findings.

Difficulties with Genetics Contribution:

To conclude this chapter, I need to mention that contributing behaviour to genetics isn't easy.

In fact, it's very difficult and behaviour will NEVER be down to genetics exclusively, because behaviour is the result of multiple genes and environmental factors interacting with each other.

Additionally, it's difficult to pinpoint what genes and environmental factors contribute more to the behaviour than others.

However, the most important thing you need to remember is all this genetic research is correlational.

We cannot establish a cause and effect relationship from this research.

Quantitive Genetics:

This is further supported by the fact that most human behaviours is between 30% to 60% genetic. Leaving a lot of room for environmental factors to influence our behaviour.

Furthermore, these genetic estimates vary by tested population, the timing and the environment.

For example, it's quite possible to find testing like depression in 2010 in Norway is 60% genetic but ten years later depression might be 45%.

That's a fictional example but you get the idea.

CHAPTER 6: CHROMOSOME ABNORMALITIES AND DISORDERS

Continuing on from the last chapter, we know how typical genes impact our behaviour, but what happens when things go wrong?

These are the results of genetic disorders.

So, normally a sperm and an egg have 23 chromosomes each and each sperm and egg only has one pair of a gene. And as much as I would love to go into the biology of genetics. I must remember this is a biological psychology book, not a biology one.

Genes and Behaviour Traits:

Returning to the theory side of genetics, the question of what alleles, versions of a gene, assert influence depend on several factors.

For example, if the genes are dominant or

recessive and if they're homozygous, a person has identical alleles on the Z chromosome, or heterozygous. This means the person has unmatched alleles on the 2 chromones.

Some other factors that influences which gene asserts influence are:

- Immediate- when both alleles are expressed as an equal force.
- Genotype- what alleles and focus at the gene locus for specific trait
- Phenotype- what you look/ behave like as a physical entity.

Chromosome Abnormalities:

There's a wide range of genetic conditions. Such as: a Trisomy condition is when a person has one or more extra chromosomes. Like Down's syndrome because they have an extra chromosome 21.

This is caused by an error in cell division and this isn't usually genetic.

In addition, there are monosomy conditions where a person only has one of a given chromosome.

On the whole, these conditions tend to be very rare because cells without a pair tend to die very quickly.

Types of Genetic Conditions:

There are four types of genetic conditions, people can suffer from and we'll look at these in the next few sections.

Autosomal Domaint:

These conditions only need the abnormal gene from one parent to be inherited and this condition can occur in either sex.

Like: Huntington's disease

Autosomal Recessive:

Since this is a recessive type of genetic condition, you need to 2 abnormal genes for this condition to develop.

If you only have one abnormal gene then you'll become a carrier.

Sex-linked Dominat:

This condition is a bit more interesting because you need a single abnormal gene on the X chromosome for these types of conditions to develop.

However, the interesting thing about these conditions is that all affected males pass on the disorder to all daughters but not to their sons.

Sex-linked Recessive:

Our last type of genetic disorder requires you both to have an abnormal gene and more men than woman show these types of conditions.

Although, if a father has a sex-linked recessive condition, they'll have a 100% healthy son but a carrier daughter. As well as the chance of female of these conditions is very rare.

Turner's Syndrome:

One example of a genetic condition is Turner's Syndrome where a girl only has one X chromosome and no second X or Y.

This affects 1 in 2,500 girls and there is no known cause but it is thought not to be genetic.

Genetic Conditions Extra:

Some disorders happen because of a mutation in the genes.

Others happen only when a mutation occurs.

Some other conditions only happen when many genes interact together.

Whilst other conditions only reveal themselves when the genetic and environmental or lifestyle factors interact. This is very common in mental health conditions.

CHAPTER 7: EVOLUTION

I will happily testify that I love evolution. I find it amazing how over time we can change and adapt ourselves to meet our needs, and I love to explain or think about how animals evolve.

I know that my example isn't psychology-related but let's talk about giraffes. They evolved; in shortest terms; because they needed to reach the treetops with the best leaves as other animals ate the lower leaves. So, the giraffes with the smaller necks died off and starved meaning that only the long-necked giraffes got to pass on their genes to the next generation.

Anyway, taking a step back evolution is the process of were organisms change generation to generation because of the transmission of inheritable characteristics.

In simplest terms, evolutionary psychology aims to apply the theory of evolution. Which focuses on how organisms evolve to maximise their chances of survival and passing on their genes to the next generation and how behaviour has evolved.

The behaviour that we will be focusing on is disgust. One of the most basic forms of emotion that are reproduced when we are repulsed from something unpleasant.

Curtis, Anger and Rabbie (2004):

In the experiment, researchers published a questionnaire on the BBC science website that was completed by over 77,000 people in over 165 countries.

After a final data clean, they had a sample of 44,000 left. You were cleaned if you watched the documentary the questionnaire was advertised on since you could have been alerted to the hypothesis.

The first set of questions were demographic questions. Like: sex, age and country.

Next, they were shown 20 photos and they were told to rate them from 1 (not disgusting) to 5 (very disgusting).

14 photos were disease-based and the other 6 were less diseased based.

Results showed that the results were consistent across all cultures.

Disease-based photos were found more disgusting. For instance: people found the organic-looking liquid more disgusting than the chemical looking one.

Female found disease based photos more disgusting than men.

There was an age-based decline in the sensitivity in disease salient stimulus.

The last question asked who was you be least likely to share a toothbrush with from a range of options. The least likely was the postman and the more likely was the spouse. Showing disgust is found more in strangers.

All supporting that disgust evolved as a defence against disease.

Critically Thinking:

The study is very valid as it used people from different cultures showing that the behaviour is universal. This adds credibility to the findings.

However, this study uses culture and makes the argument that disgust evolved as a universal behaviour. But doubt is cast on this because it doesn't take into consideration cultural variations and if cross-cultural considerations are observed for a basic phenomenon that is thought to be universal; like the origins of disgust; then this weakens the evolutionary argument.

In other words, if we take fear as a basic emotion. The native people of Alaska would take their fear of a bear and possibly use that fear to encourage them to act and probably kill the bear. Whereas if a British person was in the same position then they may take that fear and use it to increase their speed in running away.

As surely if we all evolved the same behaviour and it is a worldwide behaviour then surely it would all be the same?

Fessler (2006)

He asked 496 healthy pregnant women between ages 18 – 50 to rank 32 potentially disgusting scenarios.

For example, maggots on a piece of meat in an outdoor waste bin.

Before asking the women to rank the level of disgust in the scenarios, Fessler asked questions to determine whether they were experiencing morning sickness.

Results showed that women in their first trimester scored higher in disgust sensitivity than women in the second and third trimesters.

When Fessler controlled the study for morning sickness, the response only applied to scenarios involving food.

In conclusion, Fessler explained this in terms of the large extent of dangerous diseases, which are food-borne. Natural selection may have helped our human ancestors to be pickier with food to make up for their increased susceptibility to disease. Being pickier with food would also help humans avoid diseases that could harm unborn offspring, and thus, threaten the species.

Critically Thinking:

This study effectively explains how disgust evolved and how it helped us to survive.

Although, a more general criticism of evolutionary psychology is that some critics say that this study of psychology uses 'post-hoc' reasoning. Taking an already existing phenomenon and trying to create an explanation for this. Therefore, in reality, disgust might not have had evolved and we could only be thinking this because we're trying to create an explanation for it.

Conclusion:

While I love evolutionary theory, I will stay focused and do this conclusion.

In conclusion, evolution can affect human behaviour because it can cause humans to develop emotions and other behaviours that give us a better chance of survival and thus passing on our genes to the next generation.

For example, disgust was evolved as a defensive technique against illness so humans wouldn't get sick and die and be unable to reproduce and not guarantee the survival of the species.

PART TWO:
THE NERVOUS SYSTEM:
NEUROTRANSMITTERS,
HORMONES AND
PHEROMONES

CHAPTER 8: HISTORICAL THOUGHTS ON THE NERVOUS SYSTEM

At university in the grand lecture theatre where I had the lecture on the Nervous System, I remember being very interested in the history of not only psychology but the history surrounding the brain and the nervous system.

Due to the history alone explains a lot about past beliefs and how far we've come in our thinking.

So what did our ancestors think about the brain?

What did they believe the 1.4 kg organ that consumes 20%-25% of our energy do?

Of course, we know that the brain creates consciousness, judgment, thought, memory and emotion, but our ancestors did not.

Aristotle: (382-322 BC)

Our first historical figure is Aristotle who believed the brain was a place to cool down the blood as well as the brain received 15% of our energy.

In addition, he believed that the heart was the better candidate for behaviour.

Hippocrates (460-377 BC)

Whereas Hippocrates who is regarded as the Father of modern medicine believed that the mind didn't reside in the brain, but the mind resided in the 'essences of life' in the blood.

Galis (AD 129-200):

Moving onto more modernish times, Galis was starting to think along the right lines as he believed that mental activity was formed in the cerebral ventricles. This is an area in the brain.

Furthermore, he believed that the cognitive process of thinking involved the flowing of fluids.

Vesalius (AD 1514-1564)

This was partially supported by Vesalius when he dissected nerves and began to direct focus on the solid parts of the brain.

To learn how the brain impacts our behaviour.

Descartes (AD 1595-1650)

Lastly, the philosopher Descartes believed that the brain affected the body through various mechanisms as well as the brain communicates with the body through nerves.

Whilst, Descartes might have been correct or at least partially right about the above, he was definitely being ambitious when he believed that the brain interacts with the soul through the pineal gland.

CHAPTER 9: THE BRAIN, ANATOMY AND THE NERVOUS SYSTEM

So far in this book, we've looked at a lot of different things with the nervous system mentioned a lot but none of these chapters really tell us how the nervous system works.

Resulting in this chapter being dedicated to such a question.

Background:

I have to admit one benefit of updating books is I get to see what needs redoing and explaining.

So, I wanted to mention that a neuron is a special type of cell in the nervous system. The body uses to transmit nerve impulses (a type of electrical impulses) around the body. And there are tons of these in the human body.

In the Spinal Cord alone there are around 1

billion neurons, the Cerebal Cortex there are 12 to 25 billion neurons, and the Cerebellum has around 70 billion neurons.

One of the reasons why neurons are specialized and unique is because they have long spiny bits coming off them called dendrites. As well as some of these have dendrite pines that branch out even further. This increases the surface area and end of neuron called the presynaptic terminal.

Furthermore, neuron cells contain:

- Membrane- this controls what goes in and out of the cell.
- Nucleus- think of this as the control centre for the cell.
- Mitochondria- this is where respiration happens that produces energy for us.
- Ribosomes- this makes proteins.
- Endoplasmic reticulum- a network of tubes that guides new protein to another location.

Central Nervous System:

This nervous system is one of the most important as this system involves the brain and the spinal cord, as well as different brain areas, are involved. Such as:

- The Cerebral Cortex is involved in touch, vision, hearing and more.

- The Cerebellum is involved in co-ordination, muscle movement and balance.
- The brain stem relays information and connects the brain to the spine.

The Spinal Cord:

The Spinal Cord consists of nerves that connect the brain to the neurons in the body and not surprising, it's located in the spinal column.

Also, it receives sensory information from the sensory neurons in the body and it sends out signals to the motor system.

In case of heat, the sensory neurons would tell the spinal cord you were touching something hot. Then this would be passed onto the brain.

Afterwards, the spinal cord would send out a signal telling your hand to move.

The Spinal cord consists of grey matter. This is located in the centre of the spinal cord and densely packed with cell bodies and dendrites. As well as the white matter that is composed mostly of myelinated axons that carry information from the grey matter to the brain or other areas of the spinal cord.

Automatic Division of the Nervous System:

Very cleverly, the . Nervous System has two subsystems that help us to prepare for action and calm us down after the fight, flight and freeze response and other situations.

There are called the:

- Sympathetic system- prepare for action.
- Parasympathetic- calm down.

As a result of this, both of these systems are complimentary as well as both these systems are constantly active to varying degrees.

And if you're wondering if there's anything in particular that actives one system over the other, this is a difficult question to answer because many stimuli arouse both systems.

The Brain Lobes:

Building upon what we learned in the localisation chapter, the brain is separated into different lobes that have different functions.

For example, the temporal lobe is associated with memory, language and emotion.

Whereas, the parietal lobe is associated with reading and writing.

The function of Glia:

Glia are a type of brain cell.

It's only recently that we are beginning to understand their complex role in the brain and we still have a long way to go.

Some roles include: nourishing the neurons and controlling the process and brain development as these cells act as guidewires for the migrating brain cells.

Types of Glia Cells:

- Astrocytes- help synchronise the activity of wrapping around the presynaptic terminal and taking up chemicals released by the axon.
- Microglia- this removes viruses, fungi and other microorganisms that could harm the neurons.
- oligodendrocytes & Schwann cells build the myelin sheath that surrounds the axons of some neurons.
- Radial glia- these guides the migration of new neurons and the growth of their axons and dendrites during embryonic development.

All-or-Nothing Law:

When a neuron fires it will apply the All-or-nothing Law stating that it will or will not fire as there is no in-between so it will always fire at the same strength. Regardless of the strength of the trigger mechanism.

We tell the differences by measuring the rate they fire at but different types of neurotransmitters can affect the rate of firing.

Such as, an excitatory neurotransmitter increases the rate of fire whereas an inhibitory decreases the rate of fire.

A single neuron can have multi inhibitory and excitatory neurotransmitters in it, so the action potential depends on the sum of the neurotransmitters.

Brain-Blood Barrier:

I wonder what protects our brain from toxins?

Well, Mayhan may have an answer for us.

Mayhan (2001) discovered that a tightly jointed layer of neurons over the brain cells and acted as a filter for toxins trying to enter the brain.

This is called the blood-brain barrier.

A Quick Note on Synapses:

In the human body, there are two types of synapses; the gaps between neurons; chemicals synapses and electrical synapses.

But why have two types?

Well, compared to electrical synapses, chemical synapses are:

- Slower
- More abundant
- More precise

This results in the chemical synapses giving us more control and control is important because if every neuron was stimulated then eventually, we would max out.

Myth-Busting:

THERE'S NO TRUTH TO THE MYTH THAT YOU ONLY USE 10% OF YOUR BRAIN AT ANY ONE TIME.

CHAPTER 10: THE THREE MAIN BRAIN DIVISIONS

Over the course of this chapter, we're going to look at the three main divisions of the brain and how they impact our behaviour.

<u>The Three Main Divisions Of The Brain Are:</u>

- The Hindbrain
- The Midbrain
- The Forebrain

<u>The Hindbrain:</u>

The first division of the brain, we'll look at is the Hindbrain and this is located at the posterior (back) portion of the brain.

Furthermore, this is made up of the Medulla, Pons and Cerebellum.

The Medulla:

This part of the brain is located just above the spinal cord and it could be thought of as an enlarged extension of the spinal cord.

However, this is a vital part of the brain because it's responsible for vital reflexes. For example, heart rate, breathing and vomiting.

Hence, damage to the medulla is fatal.

Finally, cranial nerves allow the medulla to control sensations from the head, muscles and many other parasympathetic outputs.

Pons:

Located on each side of the medulla, the Pons contain nucelli for several cranial nerves and along with the medulla, it contains the reticular formation and raphe system.

These work in conjunction to increase arousal and alertness in other parts of the brain.

Cerebellum:

Whenever I see this brain area in a picture, I often think of it as a little brain stuck on the back.

So, the Cerebellum has many deep folds and it helps regulate motor movements, balance and coordination, and it's important for shifting attention between auditory and visual stimuli as well.

The Midbrain:

Continuing with our look at the brain, the Midbrain is located above the Hindbrain and below the Forebrain, and it's comprised of the Tectum.

Tectum:

The Tectum contains the Superior, important for the visual reflex function, and Interior Colliculi. This is important for the auditory reflex functioning.

Additionally, this is located on each side of the tectum and processes sensory information

Lastly, the Tegmentum is an intermediate level of the midbrain containing the nucleus for cranial nerves and part of the reticular formation.

Forebrain:

The final main division of the brain is the forebrain and this is the most anterior (forward) and enormous part of the brain and it consists of two hemispheres, the outer cortex and some subcortical regions,

We know these outer portions by the term 'cerebral cortex'.

Each side of the forebrain receives sensory information, and it controls motor movements from the contralateral side of the brain.

Contralateral means the information is processed in the opposite hemisphere it came from.

Like: information from the right eye is processed in the left hemisphere.

Substructures of the Forebrain:

One substructure, if you want to call it that, of the forebrain is the Limbic System and it consists of other interlinked structures that form a border around the brainstem.

Including, the olfactory bulb, hypothalamus, hippocampus, amylda, and angulate gyrus of the cerebella cortex.

This system is associated with motivation, emotions, memory and aggression as well as drives.

Other subcortical structures of the forebrain include:

- Thalamus- This is the relay station of the sensory organs and the main source of input into the cortical.

Most sensory information goes here first then the cerebral cortex prolongs and magnifies inputs.

- Hypothalamus- also has widespread connections with other subcortical areas and midbrain and it conveys messages to the pituitary gland to release hormones. This brain area is associated with motivated behaviours, sexual behaviours and activity levels.
- Basal Ganglia-this is associated with the planning of motor movements, aspects of memory, and emotional expression.

This brain area is damaged in conditions like Huntington's and Pakington's disease.

- Hippocampus- this area is Latin for seahorse and it's critical for storing certain kinds of memories.

Finally, the Forebrain contains a structure called Ventricles. These are liquid-filled cavities that are filled with cerebrospinal fluid. To protect the brain against the shock of the head moving, to support the weight of the brain by providing buoyancy and it provides the brain with a reservoir of hormones and nutrients.

Final Note:

I couldn't find a place to add this in the book but during my time at university, I struggled with the term Ventral.

In case, you're having the same trouble, ventral

means towards the stomach.

CHAPTER 11: NEUROTRANSMITTERS

For me, this is where we start to get into 'proper' biology because this chapter and the next chapter which is on hormones are vital forces behind various behaviours.

Let me explain…

Neurotransmitters are chemical messengers that are released into the synaptic gap; the space in between two neurons.

Steps in Synaptic Transmission:

If we dive into synaptic transmission, as it is a vital process to so many mechanisms and behaviours in biological psychology, we can learn it happens in the following way.

Firstly, the presynaptic terminal (the end of the neuron the impulse is coming from) makes small amounts of the neurotransmitter then an action potential causes calcium to enter. Releasing neurotransmitter.

Then the neurotransmitter moves from the high concentration to the low concentration (also known as diffusion) across the synaptic gap to the other terminal. As well it binds to the receptor and some of it is absorbed.

Afterwards, the neurotransmitter separates from the receptor and transporter proteins are released. Resulting in the reuptake of the neurotransmitter.

Now I could go into the more complex dynamics of how a neuron work and how a neurotransmitter is used, and I could go into this at depth.

However, the point of this book is to explain concepts simply so that's what I'll do.

Therefore, transferring information in a neuron is partly chemical and electrical.

The electrical part comes from the electrical impulse that moves the information through the neuron.

When it gets to the end of the neuron where the synapse is a neurotransmitter gets released and then the neurotransmitter diffuses (moves) across the gap and then it gets absorbed by the other neuron. Or it can get reabsorbed into the neuron it was released from. This is called reuptake.

Crockett et al (2010)

Our first study looks at the effects of serotonin; a neurotransmitter responsible for our mood and sleep cycle; on good social behaviour.

In this experiment, the researchers got 30 healthy volunteers and split them into two groups. The first group was given a dose of citalopram. Which is a Selective Serotonin Reuptake Inhibitor. (SSRI) This meant that the neuron that released the serotonin couldn't reabsorb it. This, in turn, boosted its concentration in the synaptic gap and prolonged its effects.

Then the second group was given a placebo; a chemical they thought was the SSRI, but it wasn't.

Afterwards, the two groups were given the 'Trolley Problem' this is a scenario where you are given the choice of interfering or doing nothing to stop a runaway trolley from killing five people.

Although, the two groups were given two scenarios. In the first; the Impersonal Scenario; they could pull a lever, and this would put the trolley on another track, and this would kill one person.

In the second; the personal scenario; the participant could actively choose to push a man off a bridge to save the five men.

In both of these situations, the choice is to kill one man to save five, but in the personal situation, the choice of killing is more direct and more emotionally aversive as an act.

The results for the two groups shown no differences in the choices for the impersonal situation.

Although in the personal situations the people that were given the citalopram were less likely to interfere and push the man off the bridge.

In conclusion, citalopram reduces the acceptability of personal harm to people. This is in a sense promotes good social behaviour (prosocial behaviour) so increased levels of serotonin may cause people to be more opposed to the idea of inflicting harm to another.

Overall, this study shows that neurotransmitters affect our behaviour as this can promote prosocial behaviour.

Critically Thinking:

The study was well controlled as it has a group that was given a placebo, so it was clear if the experimental group; which was the group given the SSRI; was affected by the citalopram. As you can compare the effects of the SSRIs against the placebo group.

On the other hand, the dose given to the participants was higher than in the bloodstream, but with there being over 100 different neurotransmitters in the body. How can we say that serotonin is the neurotransmitter responsible? Or could it be a mixture of several?

Fisher, Aron and Brown (2005)

In this experiment, they got 17 people who reported themselves as 'intensely in love' and did a brain scan on them in an fMRI (functional Magnetic Resonance Imaging- further information in the last chapter) and got them to do some tasks.

Firstly, the participants got to look at a photo of a loved one for 30 seconds, then for 40 seconds they were required to count back from a number, for the next 30 seconds they got to look at an image of an emotionally neutral friend and for the last 20 seconds, they counted back again. They repeated this six times for a total of 720 seconds.

The results showed that when looking at the photo of the loved one there was increased activity in the dopamine; a neurotransmitter involved in the feelings of romantic love; rich areas of the brain. More specifically in the Ventral Tegmental Area which is apart of the so-called dopaminergic pathway. This is a reward system for pleasure and motivation in the brain.

In conclusion, the neurotransmitter dopamine is involved in the feelings of romantic love.

So next time you go to kiss or hug your partner think of all that dopamine being released.

Critically Thinking:

The study was effectively designed so that the counting back exercise allowed the brain's activity to go back to 'normal' before the showing of each type of photo. Thus, this allowed the increase in brain activity to be clearly linked to the type of photo being shown.

Nevertheless, how can we be sure that those dopamine-rich areas of the brain only release dopamine? Is it possible that they release smaller amounts of other neurotransmitters and it's, in fact, the combination of this cocktail that creates the feelings of romantic love?

What do you think?

Conclusion:

Overall, neurotransmitters can affect behaviour for many reasons. For instance: they can increase prosocial behaviour, or they can make us feel romantically in love with someone.

CHAPTER 12: SYNAPTIC TRANSMISSION

Building upon the last chapter, the nerve pulse is the electrical message that is transmitted down the axon of a neuron and interestingly not only is this transport quick but there's no loss of energy as it travels. Due to the energy regenerates as it travels along the axon. As well as the electrical currents in the body reflect the flow of ions.

Nonetheless, the cost of not losing energy is the time delay between the stimuli and the time it arrived in the brain.

You can think about this in terms of when people say "That's a bit of a delayed action,"

Normally, when people say this you're mocking you but in reality, this could be a great example of this time delay.

The history of Synapses:

I never think it hurts to have a quick look at history because Charles S. Sherrington studied reflexes and his observations allowed him to infer the properties of synapses.

Without him, our understanding of biology would be weaker!

For example, he found the transmission through a reflex arc is slower than transmission through an equal length of the axon. Resulting in Sherrington concluding that some processes at the synapses delay transmission.

More on the All-Or-Nothing Law:

Moreover, if you remember the All Or Nothing law, you know the neuron either fires or it doesn't and there's no in-between.

So, for that to happen, the neuron has to reach -70mv and this triggers an action potential.

Meaning the voltage-gated sodium channels open.

Resulting in an explosive rush of positively charged sodium ions into the neuron and a reduction in the polarisation.

This makes the inside of the neuron become

positive and at a certain threshold (somewhere around -30mv) the sodium channels are quickly closed.

Making the neuron return to its resting state by the opening of potassium channels.

Afterwards, there's an outflow of potassium due to the concentration gradient and this takes the positively charge ions with them.

Personally, I recommend looking up the action potential online for the sole purpose of seeing the accompanying graph that shows what happens to the voltage during this process.

Finally, action potentials need to travel down the axon of a neuron but in axons, that are covered in a myelinated coating, the action potential can only occur in the nodes. These are, for lack of a better term, gaps in the coating.

Also, this transmission in myelinated axons is faster than in unmyelinated axons. Since the action potential can 'jump' node to node. Instead of having to travel all the way down the axon.

CHAPTER 13: BIOLOGICAL BASIS OF DRUGS: ALCOHOL, COCAINE, NICOTINE AND MORE

This has to be one of my favourite biological psychology topics because looking at the effects of drugs on behaviour means we can apply all this knowledge to our everyday life. Since drugs are a massive problem in the world.

Therefore, drugs can either facilitate (agonists) or inhibit (Antagonist) synaptic transition.

The Case of Epilepsy:

This condition is a great way to look at the effects of drugs because epilepsy, which causes seizures, are caused by abnormal electrical signals in the brain.

Thankfully, they can be treated with Antiepileptic drugs. (AEDs) These reduce the likelihood of a seizure by alternating or reducing the excessive electrical activity in neurons. As well as different AED works in different ways and have different effects on the brain.

In more detail, these drugs work by attaching themselves to the surface of the neuron.

Afterwards, they affect the neurotransmitter responsible for sending the abnormal messages to the brain.

For example, some AEDs affect the sodium channels where they bind themselves to sodium channels on neurons. Like: phenytoin and Lamotrigine.

Whereas other AEDs block calcium channels. Like: topiramate and Lamotrigine.

Dopamine and Mental Health:

Another way how neurotransmitters can impact behaviour is by causing mental conditions, and I talk about this topic a lot more in Abnormal Psychology 3rd Edition.

But the levels of dopamine in the body can have a number of effects on our behaviour. For example, too little dopamine can cause:

- Tremor and ability

- Feeling lethargy and misery as seen in depression.
- Cravings and withdrawal
- Lack of attention and concentration as seen in ADHD

This can be seen in Methylphenidate (Ritalin) as it blocks the reuptake of dopamine but in a more gradual and more controlled way. This is often prescribed for people with ADHD. Meaning this boosts the concentration of dopamine in the body. Allowing the dopamine levels in the body to return to 'normal' levels.

Also, addictive substances increases dopamine activity in certain areas of the brain as seen in "the reward pathway" as mentioned in Aron, Fisher and Brown (2005)

Whereas, too much dopamine in the body can cause:

- Hallucinations and paranoia like in Schizophrenia.
- Uncontrolled speech and movement like in Tourette's.
- Agitation and repetitive action as seen in OCD.
- Over excitement and euphoric like when people are experiencing mania.

Additionally, almost all abused drugs stimulate dopamine release in the nucleus accumbens as well as stained busts of dopamine inhibit cells that release the neurotransmitter GADA.

This is thought to be one of the causes of Schizophrenia. Please see Abnormal Psychology 3rd Edition for more information.

Although, something I love about psychology is sometimes pieces of facts contradict each other. Sometimes a lot, sometimes only slightly.

For example, activity in the nucleus accumbens probably contributes more to the 'wanting' of a drug than people actually liking it. Yet it has a role in both.

This is supported by the fact, addition is based heavily on someone wanting a drug as the amount of pleasure decreases during addiction.

Alcohol:

Alcohol and its effects are well known and people love it.

Personally, I don't drink because of its taste let alone its side effects.

However, alcoholism is a problem that's going to be the focus of this section.

Therefore, alcohol is a drug that has long historical use and is used widely throughout the world. As well as alcoholism or alcohol dependency is the continued use of alcohol despite medical or social harm even after a person has decided to quit or decrease drinking.

For example, if a person has decided to give up alcohol but they can't. Then chances are they have an alcohol difficulty.

And if you're read my Abnormal Psychology or Clinical Psychology book then you know I prefer the term condition or difficulty over the term problem. Since that word can be as damaging as the condition itself.

Furthermore, alcohol has a number of physiological effects:

- Inhibition of sodium across the member
- Expansion of the surface of the membranes
- Decrease serotonin activity

This is one reason why alcohol is a depressant.

- Enhanced response by GAGDA receptor
- Blockage of Glutamate receptors
- Increased dopamine activity

To treat addiction, Antabuse, this blocks the conversion of acetaldehyde to acetic acid, and methadone are used but many people do not respond to other treatment, so medication has been used to reduce cravings instead.

Surprisingly enough, alcoholism isn't just one type. In fact, there are two different types of alcoholism and compared to type 1, type 2 alcoholism starts faster, sooner, usually more severe, and it affects more men than women.

Causes of Alcoholism:

There are several causes of alcoholism, including cognitive and social factors, but in terms of biological causes. There are genetic influences on alcoholism because genes have an impact on impulsiveness, responses to stress and overall calmness.

Yet some risk factors for alcoholism include:

- Family history
- Feeling low intoxication after moderate drinking
- Immense stress relief after drinking

Nicotine:

We all know this drug from cigarettes and personally, I can't stand the smell and I just don't like the idea of smoking. But that's just my opinion.

So, nicotine works by exciting acetylcholine receptors, and this includes the ones on axons terminals that release dopamine into the nucleus accumbens.

In short, nicotine excites the receptors that

release dopamine. Making you feel good.

Meanwhile, this inhibits the release of GADA and this normally stops the release of dopamine into the body.

Think of this as a control measure to prevent you from feeling too great.

Other Drugs:

Whereas opiate drugs stimulate endorphins receptors.

Although, I just had a funny thought that you can get the same simulation and release of endorphins by exercising since it triggers the release of endorphins.

In addition, hallucinogens act by stimulating certain kinds of serotonin receptors.

Cocaine:

As a quick final note on the Nervous System and how it can impact our behaviour, I wanted to quickly tell you about cocaine and how it impacts the body.

Firstly, cocaine targets the following 3 neurotransmitters:

- Dopamine
- Serotonin

- Norepinephrine

Then cocaine blocks the neurons so the reuptake of the neurotransmitters can't happen.

In turns, this increases the concentration and prolongs the effects of the neurotransmitters.

In other words, making you feel great.

However, then as the cocaine loses its effects you start to suffer from withdrawal symptoms, and you start to feel bad.

Afterwards, people can become addicted to cocaine as they love the feel of that perceived high but the process of addiction has massive consequences for the individual, their loved ones and their community.

Although, I must note that the process of addiction is an interesting read so if you want to learn more about addiction then please check out my Health Psychology book for more information.

CHAPTER 14: HOROMONES

Hormones are chemical messengers released into the bloodstream to target organs and they are released by the Endocrine System. This is the name given to the system of glands that secrete (release) the hormones into the bloodstream.

Personally, I find the functions of hormones really interesting as there are so many different types and they all perform interesting and key functions for the body and our behaviour.

Let's take melatonin for example. It's a hormone that is involved in the sleep cycle and it's used in the treatment of ADHD.

But for this introduction to the world of hormones, we'll be focusing on the role of oxytocin and Adrenaline.

Oxytocin is a hormone produced in the hypothalamus in the brain and it's released by the pituitary gland also in the brain. It's known for its role in social interaction and sexual reproduction.

In addition, oxytocin is released during breastfeeding and it's important in establishing the bond between a mother and her child.

Romeo (2014)

In this study the researchers intra-nasally sprayed (sprayed a substance up their nose) 16 dogs were either with oxytocin or a placebo.

Afterwards, the dogs were placed in a room with their owner and another dog. The owner was told not to actively engage with the dog and to move their chair every ten minutes to predetermined points.

Four cameras recorded the behaviour of the dogs for an hour session.

The results of the recordings were checked against a behavioural checklist and they have shown that the dogs that were sprayed with oxytocin showed more affiliate behaviour. This was defined as licking and body contact, as well as the other shown more approach behaviour.

Furthermore, blood tests revealed that the effects of the oxytocin were bidirectional as the oxytocin encouraged more affiliate behaviour then this caused more oxytocin to be released and so on.

In conclusion, oxytocin plays a role in maintaining social bonds in mammals in a non-reproductive context.

Critically Thinking:

The experiment was controlled well as they had a placebo group to measure the results of the oxytocin group against, so we know that oxytocin does play a role in social bonds as it outperformed and had different effects to the placebo group.

However, the level of oxytocin was higher than the levels naturally found in blood, so is the effect of oxytocin really this strong in reality? Or did the experimenters get these results because of the high dose of oxytocin the dogs received?

Schacter and Singer (1962)

Adrenaline is the hormone responsible for the fight or flight response which occurs, in short, when we're emotionally aroused because of danger and we must make the choice of fighting the threat or running away, or sometimes we simply freeze.

In this experiment, the researchers got the participants that were all-male university students and divided them into four groups. All groups thought they were getting an injection of victims and they would take part in a vision experiment.

Group 1 was given the injection and not told about its effects.

Group 2 was given the injection and told about its effects.

Group 3 was given the injection and told the wrong effects.

Group 4 was given a placebo.

Then there were two conditions. The first condition; the happy condition; was when the group was sitting in an office with another person who was acting silly and fun.

The other condition; the angry condition; was when the group was sitting in the office with another person was acting angry.

The behaviour was observed through a one-way mirror and self-assessed reports were used as well.

The results have shown that in the happy condition, group 1 and group 3 reported higher levels of happiness than those who were informed about the effects of the injection. This could be as a result of they felt some physical change but didn't realize that it was because of the injection.

In the angry condition, group 1 subjects behaved significantly more angrily than group 2 and group 4 subjects. Probably because they knew that they were experiencing a physical change to their bodies like shaky hands, but they didn't have a reason for it.[2]

In conclusion, emotion is the result of contextual cues and physical cues that are combined with cognitive labelling.

In other words, emotion is the result of us labelling what's happening in the situation we're in and what our body is doing as well.

Critically thinking:

Internal validity was high as the researchers managed to measure what they desired.

However, the study does have ethical concerns about the deception of the study especially as the deception resulted in the emotional distress of some of the participants. Particularly in the anger condition.

Conclusion:

Much like neurotransmitters, hormones can affect behaviour for many reasons. Such as oxytocin plays many roles in the body including social bonding, and Adrenaline helps the body in the fight or flight response.

2

https://mrseplinibpsychologyclassblog.wordpress.com/2017/12/08/schachter-singer-1962/

CHAPTER 15: PHEROMONES

Now we've all probably heard of pheromones at some point. Whether in the world of perfumes or the natural world. But what exactly are they?

A pheromone is a chemical messenger that communicates information such as fertility or sexual attractiveness from one member of a species to another.

However, while there's a lot of evidence to support and prove their role in other mammals' behaviour and reproduction. Their role in humans is debatable.

This is because usually, mammals have something called the Accessory olfactory blub inside the Vomeronasal Organ. This is were pheromones are processed for their information by the brain.

But some humans have this blub and others do not and even if you do have it. It doesn't seem to be connected to the rest of the neurons system, so how could the pheromone's information be processed?

On the other hand, it's possible that there's another area of the brain that processes this information.

Now we're going to look at two contrasting studies on pheromones.

Lundstorm and Olson (2005)

In this experiment, the mood of women was measured in the presence of either a male or female experimenter after being exposed to Androstadiene (also known as AND); this is a chemical substance that is derived from testosterone.

The results showed that the woman's mood only increased in the presence of a male experimenter.

In conclusion, AND could play a role in signalling sexual attractiveness.

Critically Thinking:

While the study does support the idea that pheromones signal attractiveness. The effects of the pheromone can't be separated from the natural effect of the experiment.

So, is it possible that the woman's increased mood is because the male experimenter was naturally attractive compared to the pheromone being the reason for the attraction?

Hare et al (2017)

The study looked at where Androstadiene and Estratetraenol (EST) signalled gender and affected mate perception.

140 Heterosexual subjects completed two computer-based tests while exposed to AND or EST with a cotton bud under the nose with clove oil to mask the pheromone.

One day they would complete both activities while exposed to AND or EST and the other day they would complete the activities with only the clove oil.

The first activity was they were given five face morphs and they had to indicate gender.

The second activity was they were given photos of the opposite sex and told to rate their attractiveness on a scale of 1-10.

Results showed no difference in the gender assigned to the face morphs between the two groups.

For the second test, there was no difference between the attractiveness of the photos between the two groups.

The gender of the experimenter did not affect the results.

In conclusion, AND and EST doesn't intensify

attraction, so they don't count as human pheromones.

Critically Thinking:

The study was controlled effectively as it used clove oil to cover up the smell of the pheromone, so no one would be able to detect the differences and if they did detect a difference this could open the experiment up to demand characteristics. (when the participants think they know the purpose of the experiment and change their behaviour accordingly)

Nevertheless, this experiment is very artificial as we don't rate the attraction of people based on photos alone.

An example of this is a celebrity we take several factors into consideration about their attractiveness. Like: their money, why they're a celebrity a chef, a singer or author, their personality or what the media portrays them as and of course their attraction. Whether this would be their natural attractiveness or their artificial attractiveness. After the makeup people have played with their appearance.

Conclusion:

Consequently, pheromones play a role in behaviour as act as chemical messengers and they can increase a woman's mood, so they affect us because they increase our sexual attraction towards someone.

PART THREE:
RESEARCH METHODS

CHAPTER 16: RESEARCH METHODS

Prior to us exploring these interesting topics in biological psychology, I wanted to give us the opportunity to have a quick look at the types of research methods used.

The reason being that there are a lot of strange as well as interesting methods used in biological psychology, so hopefully this will make you familiar with the different research methods.

As I know from personal experience that a lot of people just presume that you know what an EEG is, so hopefully you'll find this section helpful.

<u>Reaction Times:</u>

This may sound like a basic research method that you or your children may have used in middle or secondary school. Yet it is still useful as it can indicate how information is processed with the purpose of this method being that it helps to identify how cognitive processes happen in neural tissue.

Computerized Axial Tomography (CAT scan):

It works by an x-ray passes through the body and it's picked up by a sensor on the opposite side and then it's analysed.

Since bone and hard tissues absorb x-rays better than soft tissues it can reveal information about the structure of the brain.

Overall, these types of scans are extremely useful for identifying precise locations or the extent of brain damage or other abnormalities.

For example:

- Tumours
- Blockages in blood flow
- Psychological disorders
- Structural abnormalities

In addition, CT scans provide much better clarify and detail than conventional x-rays and they're low intrusive. So, we don't need to stick things into people.

Which is always a bonus!

However, in CT scans, the participant is exposed to radiation as well as they have extremely poor temporal resolution since they only show structure and not brain activity. Also, they have poor spatial resolution at 0.5 cm- 1cm.

Magnetic Resonance Imaging:

When placed in an external magnetic field, some atomic nuclei like hydrogen emit energy and because the levels of hydrogen and therefore energy differs throughout the body. We can build a 3D image of the brain.

On the whole, this research method is invaluable in determining damage or abnormalities in brain areas as well as MRIs provide clearer and more detailed images than a CT scan with a high spatial resolution of 1- 2mm and it has a low intrusiveness.

As you can tell, I quite like MRIs and I would love to use one in the future.

Yet again, no research method is perfect since you can't use MRIs with people with metal plates or devices. Like: a hip replacement or a pacemaker and there's a risk of claustrophobia.

Finally, MRIs have no temporal resolution as they don't show activity.

Functional Magnetic Resonance Imaging:

It works by measuring the level of oxygenated blood in certain areas of the brain. It works how MRIs do in terms of picking up on emitted energy.

Moving onto the advantages, fMRI allows researchers to take detailed images of brain function, it has low invasiveness and high spatial resolution of 1 to 3mm.

Before I talk about the disadvantages, I know its a slightly longer list but fMRIs are a great research method.

Although, fMRIs aren't easy to use because they require a lot of technical and medical expertise and they're very expensive. My lecturer told us they cost about five hundred thousand pounds, or 750 thousand dollars.

Ouch, that's a lot!

Also, the scanners are very noisy so not everyone could use them. For example, I would hate them and autistic people might struggle as well.

Plus, interpreting the pattern of increased and decreased activity is challenging. Yet this is more of an experimental thing since Aron, Fisher and Brown (2005) found a good way to overcome this problem.

Finally, different people can use different brain areas for the same task. Depending on their previous experience with it and the results it produces is correlational. Therefore, you can't establish cause and effect.

Positron Emission Tomography:

A tracer is placed into the subject's bloodstream and it binds to molecules and it emits energy that can be traced. The person is placed in a scanner.

The more active a brain area, the more blood that's needed and the more energy is emitted.

The positives of Pet scans are they enable detailed images to be taken during a task so you can know what's happening into the brain.

Additionally, PET scans are more sensitive than CT and MRI scan, and they use colour to make it really easy to interpret them. That's why I really want to conduct a PET scan in the future.

Plus, PET scans have an okay or moderately good spatial resolution at 5 to 10mm.

On the other hand, since PET scans require a radioactive injection, there's exposure to radiation and these scans are moderately invasive.

As a result of this radiation exposure, the participant is limited to 3 scans per year. This sounds okay for most studies but if you're conducting a longitudinal study then this might not be good for you.

This is further inhibited by the number of scans in a session is limited and you must have at least a 40 second interval between the scans.

Lastly, PET scans have a poor temporal resolution as the scan takes 30 seconds to complete. Thus, if you want to see any processes, they have to be over 30 seconds.

Electroencephalography (EEG):

When large groups of neurons are activated simultaneously the electric potential is detectable on the surface of the skull.

Electrodes are attached to the surface of the skull so this can be detected.

Typically, the EEG uses the 10-2 system to placing electrodes on the participant and it measures the difference of the electric potential between the different electrodes.

Moreover, the raw EEG data isn't sensitive enough to distinguish between fine changes in mental activity, so the signals are averaged to decrease influence of random activity.

However, an EEG can be affected by physiological and environmental factors. Because I took part in an EEG study once and you needed to be careful about your movement as blinking, clenching your teeth and more. As these would create electrical potentials that the EEG would pick up, and mess up the data. Since it would record the blinking and other movements instead of the data from the task at hand.

As I've already mentioned, I like EEG studies except for the fact the conductive gel sticks in your hair so you NEED to have a shower afterwards.

Regardless of that fact, EEG and ERP studies are good for research since they're relatively cheap, they can be used on a wide range of participants and they have low invasiveness.

Well, I say that but during my EEG study, I almost got jabbed in the head with a blunt syringe as the researchers were filling the cap with the conductive gel.

Another benefit of EEG is it can be used to study brain activity over an extensive length of time and during long, complex tasks. The study I was involved in lasted for over an hour.

The last benefit is EEG has high temporal resolution because it can record processes in real-time.

Nevertheless, like always EEGs aren't perfect because they only allow you to allude to which brain areas are activated and their functions, as well as EEGs have low spatial resolution.

Magnetoencephalography (MEG)

Our last research method in this chapter is Magnetoencephalography and this is an interesting one. Because it's a non-invasive neurophysiology technique that measures the magnetic field generated by neural activity. Especially, the small intracellular electrical currents in the neurons of the brain.

Also, this technique is closely related to EEG as EEGs records electric potential generated by neurons and MEG measures magnetic fields of the neurons.

How Does It Work?

It sounds simple since a magnetic field can pass unaffected through brain tissues and skin but the magnetic field of a neuron is extremely small.

However, the magnetic field generated by 50,000 or more neurons firing together can be detected with the highly sensitive MEG with its special devices called: Superconducting Quantum Interference Device.

Personally, I prefer its shorter version of SQUID.

There are more than 300 SQUIDs in the helmet-shaped vessels as well as each vessel is filled with liquid helium-cooled to -269 to reduce impedance.

Then it records and detects the magnetic field generated by the neural activity.

Overall, I quite like this technique because it's non-invasive, children and infants can be tested (which is a massive relief to researchers) repeated testing is possible, it has good spatial AND temporal resolution, it's silent and there's no need for electrolytes jelly so perp time is reduced.

However, using this technique is far from perfect as the MEG risks a helium shortage, it doesn't give you any structural or anatomical data and it's very expensive. Costing between £1million to 1.5 million or $1.5 to $2 million.

Finally, there can be no external magnetic field so the MEG needs to be recorded in a specially shielded room and again this costs money.

Ultrasounds:

I know ultrasound may sound like a strange research method but it's very useful for researching the structure of the brain and body. It works by (for lack of a better term) pulsing sound waves through the body and using the reflections of the sound waves. We can build a picture of the structure.

Furthermore, there are a lot of advantages to using ultrasound. For example, it has great temporal resolution of 10-30ms. Meaning we can see processes in real-time.

In addition, it has good spatial resolution at 2mm and its low cost as well as there's no exposure to radiation.

Finally, it can detect blood flow, but I think the most exciting thing for the future is 3D ultrasound are under development based on similar principles to a CT scan.

Now that's going to be interesting!

Although ultrasounds aren't perfect because ultrasound is difficult to use on patients with larger body types because the extra tissue weakens the sound waves.

Also, the waves cannot travel through bone so it can't visualise the brain after the small bones fuse together at 18 months of age.

Pathology:

Another way to study the brain is by using pathology. This is where you study the brain after death.

Several key studies have used this research method. Including, Tan (1865)

For example, this study was used to discover Albert Einstein- brain was average size but his brain area for visual and spatial reasoning was 15% larger than 'normal' and his supramarginal gyrus wasn't divided by the Sylvian fissure.

Then again, the main problem with this research method is it depends on people donating their brains.

Meaning this will bias your sample and this gives you a smaller sample to pull your participants from.

Plus, it isn't possible to establish all the needed information about their cognitive abilities as well... they're dead.

Brain Lesions and Disorders:

The final research method that we'll look at are brain lesions and this involves studying the brain of a person who has a brain lesion or disorder.

This is called a natural experiment as you aren't manipulating any variables.

In addition, if there's damage to a specific brain area then this can lead to a specific brain deficit, as well as a lack of a particular brain activity results in a change in behaviour.

By studying these lesions and the behaviour that the sufferer shows, it allows researchers to find causal links between the brain's activity and structure and the behaviour.

This is demonstrated in the next chapter along with the drawbacks of this type of research.

CHAPTER 17: HOW TO PICK THE RIGHT RESEARCH METHOD?

Of course, I'm not going to tell you what's right for your experiment or research but I want to give you a few ideas about what to look for in a research method for you.

Tomography vs Topography:

Firstly, you need to consider how you want to study the brain and the concepts of tomography and topography are helpful in this regard.

For example, tomography comes from the Greek word 'tore' meaning to 'cut' and 'slice' as well as 'graphein' from the Greek meaning to write.

In neuroscience, tomography refers to studying the brain in slices or sections.

This is used in CAT, PET and MRI scans.

Whereas topography comes from the Greek word meaning 'topos' meaning places and 'graphein' Greek meaning to write.

Meaning in neuroscience, this refers to the projection of a sensory surface. For instance, topography is used in EEG and MEG.

In other words, if you want to structure slices of the brain then you might want to choose a method involving tomography, and not topography.

EEG/ ERP vs PET/ fMRI

Again, there is no one answer to this section and you need to consider what might be useful in the experiment. Since EEG/ ERP have good temporal resolution but PET and fMRI scans have much better spatial resolution.

Thus, you would have to consider if measuring structure or processes is important to the study.

Also, you might need to consider if you want to directly measure brain activity or not. Due to EEG reflect neural activity. This is a more direct measure of brain activity. Whereas PET/ fMRI reflect chemical changes in the blood flow.

I know it's a lot to think about, but I know you can do it!

CHAPTER 18:
PSYCHOPHYSIOLOGICAL MEASURES

Building on from the last two chapters, I want to move away from research methods focusing on the brain and the methods that measure other things. For example, bodily responses.

Therefore, in biological psychology, we have 3 main systems of measuring bodily responses.

Evaluative Reports:

Firstly, we have evaluative reports. These include participants' ratings of their emotions. And no we aren't going to get into the problems with self-reported data. This includes verbal descriptions of the bodily responses and questionnaires.

Overt Actions:

Secondly, we can study overt actions. These are particularly useful because these aren't subjective like the last system but these are direct measures of the bodily responses.

For example, reaction times, measuring behaviour, measuring physiological responses and measuring the central nervous system.

Which, as we know from the last chapter, this can be tested using fMRI and EEG.

Another way to measure overt action is by measuring the automatic nervous system. Which can be done by measuring cardiac (EEG), electrode dilation and facial muscles (EMG)

Indices of Cardiovascular Activity:

Finally, we can measure activity in the cardiovascular system. For instance, you can measure:

- Heart rate and heart period
- Blood pressure
- Heart rate variability (HRV)

I had no idea what a heart period was but its the time in milliseconds between heartbeats and blood pressure is the force exerted by the blood of the vessels walls and this is typically measured in millimetres of mercury.

(Don't ask me why)

Baroreflex:

In addition, we can measure the responses from baroreflexes. This is how the body maintains blood pressure in the body.

To do this the body uses baroreceptors. These are pressure and stretch sensors in the heart, carotid and other main arteries that detect variations in blood pressure and signal to the brain the current state of the cardiovascular arousal.

We can measure this because the signals from the aorta baroreceptors are conveyed by the Vagus nucleus tractus solitary (NTS) in the brain stem, and this results in excitatory activity in parasympathetic nuclei.

HRV is the change in the time intervals between adjacent heartbeats, and these variables in the heart period in a given time are good measurements of psychophysical activity.

EDA:

Electrodermal activity (EDA) refers to variations in the electrical variations in the electrical characteristics of the skin.

During experiments, we can measure this using two methods.

Firstly, you can apply small electrical current across the skin to measure skin conductance level.

This is called as Exosomatic.

Secondly, you can record skin potential without applying external current. This is known as Endosomatic.

Measuring Skin Conductance:

Typically, the skin isn't prepared, like cleaned with alcohol, but some researchers ask participants to wash their hands.

As well as the ambient temperature and time of day are two environmental factors that should be controlled.

One reason is if you record on a hot day at midday (the hottest time of the day) the participant will sweat and this will increase impedance.

Overall, EDA measures:

- Tonic EDA- these are slow acting components and background characters of the activity. (overall, level show climbing, slow deactivation over time)

- Phasic SCRs- faster changing elements of the signal.

Personally, I found the easiest way to think about these signal types are tonic is more of a gradual line. Then phasic is a wavy signal.

Yet tonic EDA can be further broken down as:

- Slow changes & DC components

- skin conductance level (SDC)- change in the SCL are thought to be reflet general (slow) changes in automatic arousal.

Subsequently, phasic can be broken down into:

Non-specific SCRs phasic change in electrical conductivity of the skin that acraus in the absence of an identifiable eliciting stimuli.

Event-related SCRs- These are phasic changes in electrical conductivity of skin that can be attributed to a specific eliciting stimulus.

Some Challenges With EDA Generally:

Like all research methods, EDA isn't perfect because there's considerable inter-subject differences in responsibility.

Also, you can't use this technique for too long because there's reasonably fast habituation.

In other words, the body gets used to this method and it doesn't produce different results.

Eye Tracking Technologies:

In short, this research method technique tracks your eye movements and this can be used in many areas of psychology. Including cognitive and developmental psychology.

Also, this can be done by getting the participant to wear a special type of glasses or you can put a type of sensor in front of them.

Then it tracks what your eyes are looking at, for how long and it looks at pupil size as well.

Building upon this further, pupil size changes as a function of:

- Cognitive effort
- Memory
- Sadness
- Salient stimuli
- Perception of emotional stimuli
- Brightness

Consequently, there are a lot of other factors that can influence an eye-tracking study.

Eye Trackers Problems:

Additionally, eye-tracking technology is very sensitive to room and stimuli brightness (luminosity) and some studies use stimuli that are so quick that if the participant blinks they could miss what you're tracking.

Also, performance depends on:

- Eye colour
- Glasses or contact lens
- Eyelash mascara is not allowed.

I know from personal experience when I went for my eye-tracking study. I and the researcher spent 5 minutes with glasses on and off and other things to get the eye-trackers to work.

Thankfully, it did work!

Recording Facial EMG:

The final way to measure psychophysical processes is to record the activity of the facial muscles since these can reveal many things about us. For example, implicit facial cues and our implicit reactions to certain stimuli.

This is an example of Electromyography, the electrical reconducting of muscle activity.

We can record this activity by attaching electrodes to the face and focusing on the:

- corrugator supercilii- this draws the eyebrow downwards and medially, producing the vertical wrinkles in the forehead.

- Zygomaticus major- this activity occurs when the cheek is drawn back or tightened.

- Orbicularis oculi - this closes the eyelids.

Skin Prep:

As I've already said, we can only measure this by attaching electrodes but you need to prepare the skin beforehand.

In addition, I can testify to the extensiveness of skin preparation when I took part in an EEG study. Yet this is very important to getting accurate data.

Therefore, you clean the skin to remove oil, dirt, dead skin and makeup. Then the skin is usually abraded gently. Typically, with alcohol gel to sterile the skin.

Afterwards, the electrodes are placed. These are attached using double-sided adhesive tape.

Usually, you use bipolar recording as explained in the last chapter.

Next, the researchers would add the highly conductive gel between the electrode and the skin.

This is done for several reasons. Including:

- Reducing impedance (increase conductivity of the electrical signal)

- Stabilises connectivity (removes movement artifacts)

- Stability skin hydrates and conductivity

PART FOUR:
PRIMAL DRIVES

BIOLOGICAL PSYCHOLOGY

CHAPTER 19: PRIMAL DRIVES

Some behaviours we need to be driven to perform because they don't come naturally to us. For example, doing work, manual labour and other behaviour.

However, if we look at other animals we're aware of instinctive behaviours and humans are no different.

Since there are behaviours we do without being taught as well.

Therefore, over the course of the next few chapters, you're going to be exploring these behaviours. These are called: primal drives.

In humans, eating, drinking and having sex are 3 behaviours we are driven to without any external encouragement.

Also, these primal drives have a biological

underpinning. Hence, we're looking at this in this book and these biological imperatives draw a distinction between proximal and distal motivations for behaviour.

Proximal motivations are motivations that are happening right now. For example, I am hungry.

Whereas distal motivations are longer term. For instance, I'm disposed for wanting to pass on my genes.

So, we're going to cover a lot of content. Like the following:

Hunger:

- Motivation
- Hunger and satiety
- What happens when it goes wrong?

Thirst:

- Osmotic thirst
- Hypothermic thirst
- Drinking too much

Sex:

- Why have sex at all?
- The menstrual cycle
- The male cycle
- Stages of sex

- Attraction

BIOLOGICAL PSYCHOLOGY

CHAPTER 20: HUNGER

To start our look at primal drives, we need to look at hunger.

This is a fundamental part of life and if we didn't do this (or any other primal drive) we would die.

So, we know eating strategies differ by species.

Snakes eat their prey whole.

Horses eat grass.

Lizards shoot out their tongue.

As you can see, there's no shortage of ways to eat.

It's Not Easy to Study:

Nevertheless, before we drive into the topic, I need to add the process of our hunger drive is epiphenomological.

This is an example of the mind-body problem since we feel hunger but our body eats the food and this results in the psychological feeling of fullness. Meaning food isn't measured directly.

So, it's possible to survive by swallowing a tube and 'eating' without tasting or swallowing but these processes make people dissatisfied with their meals.

Another example of this strange drive is we know when to stop eating because the body, which in this case is the stomach, indicate fullness with messages sent through the Vagus Nerve. Then our mind interprets these strange bodily signals to mean fullness and we lose our drive to eat for the time being.

Interestingly, even people with no stomach still report satiety through signals from hormones in the duodenum as well as the Lateral Hypothalamus projects to many other areas of the brain. Leading to food-associated behaviours consistent with the hunger and satiety level.

Furthermore, our main motivation for hunger is we need to eat to fuel our bodies and brains to survive.

Although our motivation to eat isn't from the cerebral cortex, instead it comes from the proximal signals from our body and at least at first is instinctive.

As well as humans have evolved to feel hungry in a healthy way. As in not too much, not too little.

In addition, our hunger depends on the content of our stomach and intestines, the glucose available to our cells, our fat supplies and our health and temperature.

Since we need our fat to survive in cold temperatures and if there is not a lot of glucose available to our cells then there's potentially less glucose available for respiration to occur.

However, our appetites can be increased just by seeing a picture of appealing food. (Harmon- Jones and Gable, 2009)

This happens for a number of reasons.

<u>Hunger Signals:</u>

When we're hungry, we receive hunger signs from our stomach, fat cells, mouth, intestines and other places. These signals go to the hypothalamus. Which three areas are involved:

- Arcuate Nucleus
- Paraventricular Hypothalamus
- Lateral Hypothalamus

When these brain areas get these signals, they tell the body we're hungry so we have the drive to eat.

Additionally, the paraventricular hypothalamus (yes there are lots of them) receives signals from the arcuate nucleus and this increases or decreases our appetite accordingly. Also, it tells the lateral hypothalamus to release insulin, and it affects our appetite in other ways as well.

As you can imagine if this brain area is damaged, it can result in our hunger to be affected. For example, it can cause a loss of appetite yet stimulation causes a gain in our appetite.

Pathways:

It took me a while to think about how best to explain this to you but pathways can be thought as a series of actions to us becoming and satisfying our hunger drive.

Therefore, the pathway is activated by our taste buds and stomach after extended periods of inactivity. For example, not eating for several hours.

This leads to hunger signals to be sent to the brain.

After a while, the distention of the stomach and repeated swallowing activate the satiety pathway. Making us stop eating.

Also, people with Prader-Willi syndrome never feel full (hyperphagia) due to disruptions in their satiety network.

Neurotransmitters:

As you have probably guessed by now, neurotransmitters have a lot of impacts on behaviour and hunger is no different because neurotransmitters can make us feel full by activating the satiety pathway artificially. For instance, by using diet pills or smoking.

In terms of natural hunger and the use of neurotransmitters, when nutrients levels drop and the body gets hungry, the brain releases neuropeptide Y.

This has several functions including the regulation of food intake, as well as it's produced in multiple areas of the brain, including the hypothalamus, and acts on a variety of receptors including the Y1 receptors.

This increase in neuropeptide Y increases appetite and is thought to produce an associated change in aggression and aggressive behaviour.

Myth Busting:

In society, there is a belief that sugar causes hyperactivity and another myth that turkey causes sleepiness.

Both of these myths are unfounded.

Yet research exists that supports the ideas of eating fish enhances some people's memory and reasoning.

CHAPTER 21: THIRST

Another basic need of animals is to drink because without water we will die.

But what biology is driving us towards thirst?

<u>Osmotic Thirst:</u>

There are two types of thirsts and the most common type of thirst is osmotic thirst.

This occurs after we eat salty foods.

I like to think of this type of thirst as the best marketing trick in restaurants because they offer you salty nuts and popcorn. Making you thirsty so you buy more drinks.

Osmotic thirst works by mammals maintain a fairly constant level of 0.15M of all solutes (molecules in solution) and cells have a semipermeable membrane that doesn't allow salt to enter the cell.

Yet when we eat salty food, this causes the solute level outside the cell, in the blood, to rise. Resulting in an increase in osmotic pressure, which is the tendency for water to flow through the cell membrane to a more concentrated area.

In other words, the water from inside the cell moves to the outside of the cell to dilute the solution.

Resulting in the cells detecting a loss of water and specialised neurons fire to trigger osmotic thirst.

Meanwhile, the kidneys produce more concentrated urine to rid the body of excess salt while maintaining as much water as possible.

<u>Hypovolemic thirst</u>

The other type of thirst is hypovolemic thirst, and this comes after you lose fluids by sweating or bleeding.

This type of thirst isn't related to osmotic pressure because it's caused by the loss of fluids through sweating or bleeding, but sometimes other things can cause it.

It works by the lost water and salts need to be replaced and the neurotransmitter 'Angiotensin II' is released around the hypothalamus leading to people to crave water and salty tastes.

Another interesting fact is animals who are

experiencing this type of thirst are suddenly attracted to salty water despite being repulsed by it under normal circumstances.

A Curious Note

Krause et al (2011) found rats with strong osmotic thirst showed decreased anxiety, decreased responses to stress and increased attempts at social interaction with unfamiliar rats. Humans have not been tested for these effects.

The Brain and Osmotic Pressure:

Like everything in this book, our brains are at the front of our biological processes so the Organum Vasculum Laminae Terminalis (OVLT) and Subfornical organ (SFO) receptors detect osmotic pressure and the sodium content of the blood. As well as the OVLT receives information from receptors in the digestive tract as well. allowing us to anticipate our osmotic need before we experience it.

Moreover, when we drink, our swallowing and the distension of the stomach give the brain cues when to stop drinking unless we drink too much.

Drinking Too Much:

I know it might seem far fetched but drinking too much can kill you because Leah Betts died after drinking too much after 'ecstasy' use. As a result, it wasn't the drug that killed her, it was the amount of water she drank after taking it. She drank between seven to eight litres in ninety minutes.

The psychoactive known as MDMA can cause Syndrome of Inappropriate Antidiuretic Hormone Secretion (SIADH) as well. This makes it difficult for people to urinate and it can lead to water intoxication and hyponatremia. That's a condition where the sodium levels in the blood are very low.

Personally, I think the only way to leave this chapter is my saying, please don't do drugs!

CHAPTER 22: REPRODUCTIVE BEHAVIOURS

Since my University lecturer, this material is based on started with this note. I wanted to do the same.

The vast majority of people do have a sex drive and do want to take part in sexual activity. Whether it's homosexual or heterosexual. But there are people who don't want to, and that's perfectly okay.

<u>Sex Drives:</u>

Many species reproduce asexually without the need of a partner and our 'method' of reproduction is certainly more complicated and comparatively inefficient biologically.

Since you need to find a partner, court them, reproduce, wait for 9 months and God knows what could happen in those 9 months, then the females need to go through mind searing pain, and then you have a baby.

That's long-winded!

So why does it happen?

It isn't necessarily to help with child-rearing since many species that reproduce sexually don't share childcare (or even engage in it at all!)

Therefore, the current thinking is that we reproduce sexually because this makes us more adaptable to drastic environmental changes and less susceptible to genetic disorders.

This makes sense since if we produced asexually and we had a genetic disorder then each child we produced would have the genetic disorder.

However, if we remember the genetic condition part of the book, we know if one parent doesn't have an abnormal gene, the condition doesn't manifest sometimes.

The Menstrual Cycle:

Believe me, there's no easy way to talk about this topic but I'm taking the stance, we're all grow-ups and we're here to learn about psychology.

So, I'm going to power through this topic.

Since we're talking about sexual drives, we have

to talk about the menstrual cycle since this is a major part of the female sex drive.

Therefore, the menstrual cycle is generated by an interaction between the pituitary gland, the hypothalamus, and the ovaries.

When the last cycle ends, the anterior pituitary gland releases the Follicle-Stimulating Hormone (FSH) and it's this hormone that prompts the growth of a follicle (a small sag) in the ovary. This would allow the female to nurture an egg.

Next, the Follicle produces several types of estrogen. Like, estradiol.

Subsequently, towards the middle of menstrual cycle, the follicle builds more receptors to the Follicle-Stimulating Hormone. Making the Follicle become more sensitive to the hormone and this increases estradiol as well.

Afterwards, the increase in estradiol causes the anterior pituitary gland to release more FSH and another hormone called the Luteinizing hormone (LZ) and the two hormones combine to produce an egg.

What remains of the Follicle produces progesterone which prepares the uterus for nurturing a fertilised egg.

If an egg is fertilised both hormones continue to increase, if no egg is fertilised then both the hormones start to decline.

Overall, the female sex drive is heavily driven by this cycle and the hormones produced within it.

The Male 'Cycle'

Yes, I am as surprised as you are about this fact.

I had absolutely no idea there was such a thing before I learnt about this topic.

Anyway, testosterone is the key to the male sex drive, and this hormone increase the touch sensitivity of the penis.

During the male cycle, different sex hormones bind to the receptors in the hypothalamus. Mainly, in these three areas: the ventromedial nucleus, the medial preoptic area (MPOA) and the anterior hypothalamus.

Afterwards, the testosterone in the body acts on the MPOA to release dopamine. Making the male feel good and leading to an ejaculation over time.

Whilst my notes say something very true, it's far too blunt even for me so the male cycle tends to be more active during certain times.

Nonetheless, the male cycle isn't restricted to the

same temporal restrictions as the female cycle.

Personally, I think this highlights another strange thing about our reproductive method, because it's more effective from a biological standpoint if both the male and female cycles have the same lack or same restrictions as one another?

Castration:

Well, I have to admit this chapter looks at everything, doesn't it?

Since this is a painful topic to write about, just the thought of castration makes me want to cross my legs. I'm going to speed along with this section.

So, in case you don't know, castration is the term for the removal of the testicles.

Interestingly, when the testicles are removed, this greatly reduces the male sex drive but it doesn't eliminate it completely. Suggesting other areas of the body produce testosterone as well.

This was supported by a study where castrated male rats were found to produce amounts of dopamine in the MPOA. Yet the rats didn't release the dopamine when in the presence of a female rat and these rats didn't try to reproduce.

The Stages Of Sex

I promise you we're almost at the end of this enlightening chapter, and sex has several stages to it.

And I'm amazed someone actually spent time to dissect sex into several stages.

Don't you find that a bit odd?

The first stage of sex is the desire/excitement stage and for the most part, these are the same thing.

So, in both sexes testosterone is released and this dictates the level of excitement. Since the more testosterone, the higher the excitement.

Also, as you can probably guess it's very difficult to reach an orgasm without a high level of testosterone.

In addition, during this stage, in women the Luteinizing hormone is positively correlated with excitement as well.

The final step in this stage is dopamine is released in both sexes so they feel pleasure and nitrogen oxide as well as noradrenaline increase blood flow to the genitalia.

Afterwards, we move onto the plateau stage were the bodily responses to the sympathetic nervous system continue to increase the activity in the amygdala increases, while the hippocampus decreases.

Following on from the plateau, we reach the orgasm stage where oxytocin is released and this causes a feeling of closeness, rhythmic muscle contractions and ejaculation.

Meanwhile, the nucleus accumbens releases a very large amount of dopamine. Making us feel relaxed.

Finally, we reach the resolution stage where our heart rate and muscles relax because of the dopamine surge and the parasympathetic nervous system becomes more active to calm us down.

Although, men need a refractory period or rest at this point in the stages because men need time to produce the required amount of neurotransmitters to orgasm again.

While, women don't need a rest, so some women can experience multiple orgasms before a resolution period.

I would argue that difference is another example of our complex biological method, but I would rather move onto the next chapter.

Wouldn't you?

PART FIVE: SENSATIONS

BIOLOGICAL PSYCHOLOGY

CHAPTER 23: SENSATIONS AND PRECEPTIONS

Our senses are a vital component to us and our lives as our senses allow us to see, experience and love our lives.

Yet how do our senses work?

How do we experience the world?

Those very board questions will be our focus for the next few chapters.

What is a Sensation?

Sensation is the process of interpreting the world around us.

For example, seeing a beautiful bird or the feeling of the warm sun on our skin.

Now I must warn you that the next psychological fact does sound like science fiction, but it is what my psychology textbook said and I'll explain it better in a moment.

This process of interpreting the world requires different types of energy to be converted and placed into our brain. This conversion is called: transduction.

In all honesty, it doesn't sound like science fiction that much; it's just worded badly; as our sensory organs do pick up different energies to convert into sensations.

For instance, when you see a person, your eyes are detecting the light energy that is reflected off that person and into the eye.

Therefore, your eye converts the light energy into a format that the brain can understand. Resulting, in you seeing the person.

What is Perception?

Perception is the aggregation as well as interpretation of sensory input from our raw neural signals into more meaningful information.

In much simpler terms, perception is simply making meaningful sense of the input that we have received.

Using our previous example, our perception of the person is the meaningful interpretation of the light that was entering our eyes.

The Senses:

Over the next few chapters, we'll be focusing on each of these primary senses, but our 5 primary senses are:

- Sight- vision
- Smell- olfaction
- Touch- somatosensorial
- Taste- gustation
- Hearing- audition

However, humans and other animals have other senses as well. For example:

- Balance- vestibulation
- Pain- Nociception
- Kinesthesis- proprioception
- Temperature- thermoception
- Time- chronoception

A Quick Note on Smell:

Our sense of smell is arguably one of the most important senses as smell allows us to protect ourselves and our community from toxins in the air.

For animals in general, smell has several important roles. Such as: helping animals find food, avoid predators as well as it can provide species with a way to communicate. The chemicals involved in this communication process are called: pheromones.

However, smell is arguably the one sense that we know the least about.

On the other hand, we know that molecules travel through the air, sometimes get taken up through the nostrils and bind to the olfactory expilation. This is a mucous membrane containing the olfactory (smell) receptors. Afterwards, an electrical response is caused.

Allowing nerve impulses to reach the smell receptor area of the brain were smell receptor pulses converge (glomeruli) producing the sense of smell.

So after learning briefly about the sense of smell, let's move onto some more interesting senses.

CHAPTER 24: PSYCHOPHYSICS

Psychophysics is an interesting approach that investigates the relationship between how reality truly is and how we perceive it.

An example of a psychophysics question is: what's that amazing flavour in that cake you're eating?

This is a good example of a psychophysical question because it makes you think about what physical ingredients lead to the psychological perception or sensation of the taste.

Although, what if there were other ingredients in that cake?

How would you be able to detect them?

This is where absolute and difference threshold come in.

- Absolute threshold is the smallest amount of a stimulus that you can detect.
- The difference threshold is the small amount of a stimulus that must be increased or decreased so an individual can detect the difference.

In psychophysics, this is called: the just-noticeable difference. This is the smallest difference that an organism can reliably detect between two stimuli.

Meaning that for an ingredient or any stimulus to be able to be detected, it must be at or above the just-noticeable difference.

Laws of Psychophysics:

Just like traditional physics, psychophysics has some of its own laws including:

- Weber's law- this is the observation that the size of the difference threshold is proportional to the intensity of the standard stimulus.

This law allows us to detect if the perceiver has experienced a change or not, and it allows us to compare how sensitive difference sensory modalities are. Like: comparing the eyes and ears.

- Fechner's law- the observation that the strength of a sensation is proportional to the logarithm of a physical stimulus.

In other words, as the physical sensation increases so does the psychological sensation in a logarithm way.

However, since Fechner we know that this doesn't all ways hold up as in pain; for example; a small increase in the physical sensation can cause a massive increase in the psychological perception of pain.

CHAPTER 25: THE SENSES, THE BRAIN AND THE NERVOUS SYSTEM

As we already know from a previous chapter, the brain is made up of neurons and the all-or-nothing law states that neurons can only fire at a fixed intensity.

Meaning that there's a problem in terms of how the brain perceives sensory input, so a few ideas have been suggested.

One of these answers is anatomical coding meaning that when a particular area is stimulated; for instance; there's pressure on your arm, nerves from this brain area inform the brain to what part of the body is being stimulated.

Another answer is temporal coding. This is where the difference in neuron activity depends on the intensity of the stimulus.

For example, burning your hand would result in

more pulses per second than placing your hand in warm water.

Additionally, there are a number of brain primary sensory areas that are important for sensations:

- Vestibular cortex
- Somatosensory cortex
- Visual cortex
- Auditory cortex
- Olfactory cortex

The Nervous System:

Thankfully, over the years we have improved and come a long way in learning about how a physical sensation can lead to a psychological sensation.

For example, to explain the 'chocolate' sensory experience we could start with the physical features of chocolate. Then electrochemical and that allows us to explain the sensation of chocolate. I know it's ambitious but we'll look at the ways now.

Sensory Codes:

Each of our modalities; vision, hearing, taste and smell; has its own features and it has its own rules.

When these modalities come on through our sensory organs. They're amplifying and to amplify them they can be converted in a signal for our sensation.

For instance, how the nervous system turns the feel of a pen into neural impulses so the brain knows that you're holding a pen and not a piece of paper.

Additionally, the psychological intensity of the sensation is usually coded by the rates at which the neurons fires as well as the sheer number of neurons triggered by the stimulus.

In other words, the more neurons that fire and the quicker they fire. The greater the sensation for better or for worse.

Finally, the sensation of taste is a great example of this sensory code as the receptors for taste are located primarily on the tongue in the papillae and there are five types of receptors. Therefore, the taste of salty, sweet, sour and bitter all correspond with different patterns of neurons firing across the receptors.

CHAPTER 26: VISION

Vision is special to all of us as it allows us to experience the world in a very unique and amazing way that our other senses cannot give us.

In addition, despite my need for glasses and there is little doubt that I will need stronger glasses over the years. I still love my ability to see the world and I truly feel for the people who sadly cannot see.

How Do We See The World?

To spare you from an overly complex explanation of how we see, the simplest version of how sight works is: light enters our eye and the lens reflects the lights to the back of the eye. Where the image should form on the retina then the optic nerve transmits this information to our brain to be interpreted.

Other Parts of The Eye:

However, other key parts of the eye are important for sight. Such as:

- The fovea is located in the back of the eye and this is where our vision is sharpest.
- The blind spot is where our cells connect to the optical nerve so we can't see anything that falls here. the cornea is the surface layer of the eye and this feature bends light into the eye.
- The Iris is a band of muscle that expands and contracts to control how much light enters the eye.
- The pupil is the opening into the eye and it's controlled by the Iris.
- The lens is a feature of the eye that allows us to focus on near or far away objects.
- The retina contains different photoreceptors that are stimulated by the different qualities of lights.

Visual Deficits- Short-Sightedness:

Whilst, I am long-sighted, my dad is short-sighted, so I know that whatever type of sight condition you have. It's annoying!

In short-sightedness, this is where you cannot see things that are close to you, occurs when the eyeball 'stretches' so the image no longer forms on the retina but forms in front of it.

Causes of Short sightedness:

In an effort to discover the causes of short-sightedness, there is the near-work hypothesis. This proposes that short-sightedness is caused by working too close to the computer.

In addition, from a developmental perspective, there is the visual stimuli hypothesis that proposes that people acquire short-sightedness through a lack of so-called normal visual stimulation. This impairs optical development.

In my opinion, I am a bit confused about the latter hypothesis as from personal experience I know that my dad has had perfect vision for the past 50 years.

Therefore, if his short-sightedness was caused by a lack of 'normal' visual stimulation, then why did his short-sightedness develop so late in his development?

Finally, what I discuss in Developmental Psychology in the Sensory development section casts even more personal doubt onto this hypothesis.

When Senses Collide:

Throughout this section of the book, we've looked at several senses, how they develop and how they can impact our behaviour.

However, what happens when the senses

combine?

Interestingly, synaesthesia involves a fusion of different senses and inputs.

Some examples include:

- Graphene- colour synthesis letters and numbers are associated with different colours.
- Chromesthesia- different sounds trigger different colours.
- Auditory- tactile synaesthesia- different sounds trigger different sensations of the body.

CHAPTER 27: HEARING

I love the ability to hear and I always feel truly sorry for people who can't as I love to hear music, audiobooks, the sound of nature and more.

So I will fully admit that this chapter will be complex to some extent but in my usual style, I will tell you the information then give you a more user-friendly explanation.

I highly recommend reading the terms below before we learn about hearing:

- Cochlea- it's a coiled structure in the inner ear.
- Oval window- it's a membrane that separates the middle ear from the inner ear.
- Auditory ossicles- three bones in the inner ear that transmits the vibrations of the eardrum to the oval window.

- Basilar member- a membrane that runs the length of the cochlea. Soundwaves cause it to deform that bend the hair cells. Causing the auditory reception to be stimulated.

How Do We Hear?

Note: please free feel to jump to the section below to hear the user-friendly explanation of how we hear.

Sound waves are the energy that our brain interprets as sounds and these can differ in amplitude (loudness) and frequency, as well as these waves, set up vibrations in the eardrum.

Following this, the vibrations are transmitted across the auditory ossicles to the oval windows, whose movements create waves in the cochlea within the cochlea is the basilar membrane that contains the auditory receptors that are stimulated by the membrane's deformation.

Subsequently, the nervous system interprets the excitation from different basilar regions as different pitches.

User-Friendly Explanation:

Personally, I hate the explanation above as it's complex and filled with horrible words, but I like to give you the information in case you find it useful.

Therefore, we hear because sound waves enter

our eardrum that causes our eardrum to vibrate, and these vibrations travel throughout our hearing system to the auditory receptors. That convert the vibrations into impulses that our brain can understand and interpret into sound for us.

I hope that this explanation made sense.

CHAPTER 28: OTHER SENSES

In our last section on the psychology of sensations and perception, I thought that I would throw in a quick chapter on the other senses because these other senses are still important to us being human.

Therefore, it would be awful of me if I didn't include a quick note on our sense of pain amongst other senses.

Although, I did want to say that our senses aren't fixed. I mean that if in childhood we are very sensitive to heat then in adulthood we won't necessarily be very sensitive to heat.

Of course, this could be the case but as a result of sensory adaption, our sensitivity to heat; in this case; can decrease.

This is because sensory adaption is the process were our sensitivity to a stimulus; like heat, light or sound; declines if we're exposed to the stimulus for an extended period of time.

The Other Senses:

- Kinesthesis- the sensation generated by receptors in the muscles, joints as well as tendons this tells us about our skeletal movements.

This tells us about our movements and the orientation of our body.

For example, this sense tells us that we're moving our neck to look to our left.

- Vestibular (balance) sense- this sense uses movements of the head and allows us to know which way is up or down.

The Skin Sense:

This sense is a bit more interesting than the others because the skin sense actually has some history to it, and as I love to learn, I love history as well.

So this was perfect for me, because whilst the Greek philosopher Aristotle believed that all senses through the skin could be classed as touch.

Today we know that these senses encompass a large range of senses. For example, pressure, warmth, cold and pain.

In addition, it's not surprising that certain areas of the human body have greater sensitivity than others. For instance, sensitivity is high in the lips, genitals areas and hands.

This increase in sensitivity has many useful applications for life as well as survival.

<u>Pain:</u>

Pain is a horrible sensation but it's an important part of the human experience and as I'll tell you in a moment it is important for survival and other functions.

I know it's a pain to know that it's important, but sadly it is.

Therefore, focusing on the sensation of pain, this feeling begins with the activation of nociceptors. These are receptors in the skin that give rise to the sense of pain as they detect tissue damage as well as temperature extremes.

Furthermore, these receptors come in two types.

Firstly, you have delta-fibres that allow for the rapid transmission of information as well as these receptors give you the initial sensation of pain.

Basically, telling you to MOVE your hand away

from the oven!

Secondly, you have the C fibres that are responsible for the aching pain that remains after the injury.

However, the experience of pain is influenced by other mechanisms. Such as endorphins as well as our own neural shortcuts that can provide a 'gateway' that blocks the transmission of some signals from the nociceptors.

Preventing us from feeling all the pain sometimes.

Nonetheless, we must remember that pain is useful to some extent as it teaches us what not to do, so we can learn from our mistakes and not do it again.

This aids survival as if we get an electric shock from messing around with a toaster then the pain from the shock teaches us not to do it again. As messing around with a toaster whilst it's plugged into the wall can kill you.

Some other examples include:

- The pain from burns you get when messing around with fire.
- The pain of broken bones when you were doing dangerous tricks on your bike.

- The pain of injuries caused by hitting a car when you don't wait for the traffic lights to turn green.

PART SIX:
THE PSYCHOLOGY OF SLEEP

CHAPTER 29: INTRODUCTION TO SLEEP

I thought that I would end this book looking at sleep because we all need sleep but:

How does it work?

Why do we need sleep?

Why do we dream?

These are all interesting as well as important questions that we need to answer to be able to understand the whole point of sleep.

Because let's face it, sleep can be inconvenient as sometimes I would rather be doing something than sleeping.

However, as you will find out throughout this next section sleep is vital so it shouldn't be taken lightly.

What is Sleep?

Personally, I always find these sorts of questions to be great because 'what is sleep?' is one of those annoying questions as we know what sleep is but it's almost impossible to put into words.

Nonetheless, three definitions include:

- "Sleep is a readily reversible state of reduced responsiveness to, and interaction with, the environment."
- "Sleep is a naturally recurring state characterised by reduced or absent consciousness, relatively suspended sensory activity, and inactivity of nearly all voluntary muscles."
- Sleep represents an altered state of consciousness (Mutz, Javadi, 2017)

Although, regardless of how you define sleep it must be noted that sleep is a universal behaviour that is displayed by higher vertebrates (all mammals and birds), and some cold-blooded vertebrates.

The Circadian rhythm:

As I read these slides and passages for my university lecture, I was immediately interested in the whole sleep concept but then this strange word kept popping up.

This word or phrase was the 'Circadian Rhythm'

Which come on is a nice word to say.

So, before we continue, we need to define it.

A circadian rhythm can be defined in simple terms as a circular rhythm that the body goes through.

In terms of sleep, the circadian rhythm is our melatonin; more on than later; drops during the day as we wake up and remains low during the day and increase as we get closer to bedtime and remains high during the night.

Before it comes full circle and drops back down to lower levels in the morning.

<u>Circadian Rhythms For The Entire Body:</u>

Many bodily functions follow a circadian rhythm and these are the product of endogenous influences; influences that originate from inside the body; and exogenous influences; influences from outside the body.

Some examples of exogenous influences include:

- Light
- Temperature
- Environment

The purpose of endogenous rhythms is to keep

the working of our internal body in sync with the outside world.

This is important as the human circadian clock generates a rhythm that is longer than 24 hours when it has no external cues to refer to.

As supported by Kelley et al (1999) who studied naval officers on 18-hour shifts.

Exogenous or External Cues:

These cues rely on a stimulus to reset the circadian rhythm. This is called a Zeitgeber. (time trigger)

Although, out of all the stimulus that the human body encounters light is crucial for resetting the rhythm.

Overall, the human body runs on a biological clock that needs to reset itself and we need stimulus in order to do that.

Mechanisms of the Biological Clock:

There are 3 mechanisms involved in the biological clock and these include:

- Melatonin
- Genes that produce certain proteins
- The Suprachiasmatic nucleus (SCN)

The SCN is part of the hypothalamus and it's the main centre of the circadian rhythm for sleep and temperature.

If the SCN is damaged then this results in less consistent body rhythms that aren't synchronised to the environmental patterns of light as well as dark.

In addition, cells in the SCN fire their action potentials in a very specific rhythm that are generated by the SCN are genetically controlled.

Additionally, light resets the SCN via a small branch of the optic nerve called: the retinahypothalamus path. That travels directly from the retina to the SCN.

The way how the SCN affects sleep is because the SCN controls activity in other areas of the brain. Like the pineal gland.

The pineal gland is important as it secretes melatonin; a hormone that regulates the circadian and circannual rhythms as well as it increases 2-4 hours before bedtime.

The Genetic Basis of Circadian Rhythms:

Two genes are involved in circadian rhythms and they are:

- Timeless- this gene produces proteins called TIM.
- Period- this gene produces proteins called PER.

When TIM and PER are in high concentration, they interact with a protein (clock) to induce sleepiness.

However, if the clock gene is damaged then this can result in a reduced sleep as well as erratic sleeping pattern.

Furthermore, mutations in the PER gene can result in strange circadian rhythms.

So now that we've looked at the basics of sleep and the circadian rhythm, what happens to us when it gets disrupted?

CHAPTER 30: DISRUPTIONS TO SLEEP AND THE CIRCADIAN RHYTHM

We all hate being interrupted when we're sleeping, but what can cause our Circadian Rhythm to become disrupted and by extension our sleep?

Common disruptions of circadian rhythms include:

- Monday morning blues
- Jet lag
- Shift work

These cause disruptions to the rhythm because they result in a mismatch between the internal circadian clock and external time.

Jet Lag:

Personally, I have never been jet-lagged but from what I've read it is characterised by sleepiness during the day and sleeplessness at night.

This happens because of the mismatch between the internal and external clocks as:

- Travelling west results in 'phase-delays' to our circadian rhythms as you go to bed later and get up later.
- Travelling east results in 'phase-advances' in circadian rhythms as we go to bed earlier and wake up earlier.

Interestingly, it's easier to cope when travelling west because the day of the travelling is lengthened.

Therefore, as our endogenous cycle is about 25 hours we are better at adapting to the 'phase delay' then 'phase advances'

Shift Work:

As my dad does a lot of shift work, I know that from what my dad says shift work destroys your sleep cycle.

The reason for this is because getting up or going to bed earlier than normal is an example of phase advances.

Whereas going to bed late or getting up late is an example of phase delay.

Consequences of Shift Work:

Note: when I class the following as interesting. I mean from a psychological standpoint.

In fact, I felt quite horrified and concerned for my dad as I read this section.

Interestingly, when a shift worker's sleep cycle is disrupted by a night shift a lot of accidents tend to happen.

Some of these accidents include:

- Chernobyl occurred between 1 am and 4 am.
- Lorry accidents as most of them happen between 4 am and 7 am.
- In the USA, $77 billion are annually spent as a result of accidents and medical expenses due to shift work illness.

Although, people can get use to a new shift as Hawkins and Armstrong-Esther (1978) studied 11 nurses during a 7-night rotation and whilst their performance was greatly impaired on the first night. It was improved during the week.

Age Influences:

Age is a major determinant of sleep. As across the human lifespan, sleep undergoes a wide variety of modifications which are broadly typical for our species.

For example:

- A newborn baby sleeps for 16-18 hours throughout the day.
- A 3-5-year-old sleeps for 10-12 hours per day with afternoon naps and a long night sleep.
- A teenage needs about 8 hours per day with an increased need for daytime naps.

Sleep in Old Age:

The amount of sleep that is needed decreases to about 6-7 hours per day but:

- It becomes more fragmented.
- It's done in shifts
- It's easier to fall asleep
- More occasional night wakeups

CHAPTER 31: STAGES OF SLEEP

Before, we dive into the stages of sleep, it's important to learn how we can measure the stages of sleep because if we can't measure something then it's hardly scientific.

How Do You Measure The Stages of Sleep?

Firstly, we can measure sleep through an EEG as this allows researchers to discover that there are various stages of sleep.

Two other methods include:

- A Polysomnography that records both EEG and eye-movement. (EOG)
- An actigraphy watch- this is a recording device with a movement sensor on it called an Accelerator.

An EEG has a number of benefits to researchers as well since it's relatively cheap, low invasiveness and can be used to study brain activity over a period of time as well as it can be used on a wide variety of patients.

Stages of Sleep:

The first stage of sleep is when the person has just started 'light sleep' and this is where the brain activity starts to decline, it starts a period of relaxation and it represents about 5% of sleep time.

Secondly, you have stage 2 or the beginning true sleep and in this stage, the brain activity is more erratic with bursts of brain activity for half a second, and this true sleep makes up about 50% of sleep time.

In stage 3, you enter deep sleep so your brain activity moves to lower levels of delta waves, your heart and breathing rate drops. It represents about 15%-20% of sleep time.

Finally, you have rapid eye movement or REM sleep. This is a mixture of brain activity from stage 1 as if you're about to wake up and deep sleep as well. This odd stage represents 20%-25% of sleep time.

Brain Mechanisms of Sleep:

Personally, I do love it when there's a study to explain everything for you instead of having to listen to me ramble on about the theory.

Therefore, Constantin Von Econom (1917)

studied the brains of people who had died from Spanish flu as well as some patients had fallen into a coma before dying. While others went without sleep for days before dying.

After these two types of patients had died, Constantin performed autopsies on the brains and he found two different types of lesions. One type for each type of patient.

Firstly, he found a lesion in the 'wakefulness centre' at the posterior hypothalamus or the upper midbrain. This lesion was found in the people who had entered a coma before dying.

Additionally, he found a lesion in the 'sleep centre' for the patients who died after days without sleep.

Building upon this study, there are many structures within the brain that complete many important functions for us, and in terms of sleep these important brain areas include the brain stem and the hypothalamus.

In addition, the brain stem is very important for sleep as:

- It's where the wake centre is located.
- It receives sensory information.

Meaning the brainstem plays an essential role in maintaining the state of wakefulness.

However, if the brains stem is damaged then it can lead to a coma.

Building upon this further, the anterior hypothalamus is where the 'sleep centre' is located and if it's damaged then this can lead to sleeplessness.

CHAPTER 32: FUNCTION OF SLEEP AND SLEEP DISORDERS

Why do we sleep?

That's a truly interesting question because they say the average person spends a third of their life sleeping, so why do we bother wasting that third of our life sleeping instead of living?

This is a vital question that we need to answer.

Therefore, psychology has two theories to help us answer this question.

Evolutionary Theory:

Personally, I love evolutionary theory and you could probably tell that from our introductory chapter on Evolution.

Consequently, building upon the knowledge that we developed in that chapter, this explanation predicts that animals sleep different amounts at different time depending on when their food is most available, and they need to watch for prey.

For example, humans; at least back in the day; tended to eat cattle and other animals that grazed during the day.

Meaning that we slept during the night so we could be awake for the daytime when our food was most available.

The same is true for bats that tend to eat insects and out of all the thousands of species of bat; only 3 drink blood; and these insects tend to be out during the night.

Hence, they sleep during the day and not in the daytime.

Repair and Restoration Theory:

In my opinion, this is a common theory because I remember when I was enquiring; makes me sound smarter than I was; on the topic of sleep. It was this theory that I kept hearing.

Although, I have limited faith in this theory due to the limitations and evidence that I'll talk about later.

Therefore, this interesting theory proposes that animals need sleep to repair the brain and body after a hard day's work.

For example, a sleep-deprived human becomes irritated, dizzy and hallucinates.

To summarise, according to the theory we sleep to repair our brain and body as they become damaged after a day's work.

Evidence Against This Theory:

However, as I prelude to early there are a few negatives of the theory.

For example, there's no relationship between how hard you've worked and how much we sleep.

Meaning that if you've worked a twelve-hour shift doing intense manual labour compared to someone who hasn't worked that day. There's no evidence that the shift worker will sleep more.

This goes against the theory as that workers need to sleep more to repair the brain and body more.

Other evidence against the theory includes:

- None of these negative effects are permanent.
- Disturbances after sleep deprivation are mainly in attention tasks and not in complex cognitive tasks.
- No correlation between duration of sleep and the magnitude of performance deficits.

- Heavy physical or mental exertions increases sleep only slightly.

Improved Cognitive Functions:

Another explanation for why we need sleep could be sleep improves our cognitive functions such as memory, decision making, as well as many other functions.

This is supported by Scullis and Blivise (2015) that found that sleep disruptions result in impaired memory, cognition and attention.

Introduction to Sleep Disorders:

Whilst, this will be a quick overview of sleep disorders you will find this useful and... I'll let you keep reading.

One of the common examples of sleep disorder has to be insomnia; the inability to sleep; and it has a lot of different causes. Including:

- Noise
- Stress
- Pain
- Diet
- Uncomfortable temperature
- And more

Interestingly, when a man suffering from insomnia realised that he couldn't sleep as he hated waking up to go out for his morning jog. Then he changed the time of the jog to late afternoon. He slept fine.

So, try to find out why you can't sleep before you try and fix it.

Another cause of insomnia is the use of sleeping pills as frequent use causes you to become dependent. Leading to an inability to sleep without them. (Kales, Schory and Kales, 1978)

Note on Coffee:

Really this is a note to myself to be honest because I love coffee. I usually have a cup in the morning and a cup in the evening but after reading this I'm trying to, or at least, reducing the number of nights a week that I have a coffee in the evening.

Coffee delays the release of melatonin (Durke et al, 2015)

Other Sleeping Disorders:

Minor PG warning.

Before we dive into this last section, I must tell you about this awful sleep disorder that I personally find very interesting and it's called: Sexsomnia and I found that interesting because it's basically sleepwalking but you have sex with yourself while you're asleep.

And during my research and reading for my university degree, I came across a great example I sadly forget where I found it but this woman was telling her therapist that her marriage was breaking down because she used to have such great sex with herself during one of these episodes. She didn't want to have sex with her husband when she was awake.

Other sleeping disorders include:

- Sleep Apnoea- where people with the condition experience long periods without breathing. Unfortunately, no treatment can treat the condition fully.
- Narcolepsy- with this condition people experience attacks of sleepiness during the day. Additionally, narcolepsy is associated with a deficiency of the neurotransmitter orexin.
- Sleepwalking and sexosima- these are cases of somewhat purposeful, confused behaviours that occur during partial arousal during sleep and the person is unlikely to remember it later.

So we've answered the question of why we sleep, but the next question is: Why do we dream?

CHAPTER 33: DREAMING

The answer to the question of why we dream has a long way to go and there are a lot of different theories to why we dream.

But to simplify it all we're only going to be looking at two theories- but I would recommend looking at Freud's theory of Wish Fulfilment.

Activation-Synthesis Hypothesis:

In my opinion, this is quite a likeable theory because it makes sense and it's quite a good explanation.

According to the theory, we dream to make sense of sparse and distorted information.

In terms of brain activity, dreaming starts in the pons. Leading to the activation of many parts of the cortex. Including the amygdala which is important for emotion.

Resulting in the cortex synthesising a story from the pattern of activation.

Additionally, as normal sensory input can't compete with our own self-generated stimulation. It results in hallucinations also known as dreaming.

In other words, the theory proposes that we dream to make sense of information and it's the brain activity in parts of the cortex that create the stories that we see in dreams.

Finally, something that I like about this theory is that it can explain some of the common elements of dreams. Like: falling or not being able to move.

Neurocognitive Hypothesis:

Personally, this is another theory that I like because it involves clinical studies and it builds upon the first theory a lot better.

This theory was derived from clinical studies done with patients suffering from brain damage.

Similarly to the last theory, dreaming begins with an arousing stimulus that is created in the brain.

However, this theory adds that this stimulation is combined with recent memories and any information the brain is receiving from the senses.

Overall, the theory proposes that dreams are

similar to thinking except it happens under unusual circumstances.

As the brain is getting little information from sensory organs. It frees up other areas of the brain to create visual images.

For example, during dreaming, there's higher activation in the visual areas of the brain. Such as the parietal cortex.

This is important for visuospatial perception.

Furthermore, as brain activity in the prefrontal cortex is suppressed. It impairs working memory during dreaming. This is why we lose track of what's happening in a dream. Like: when there's a sudden change in scenario.

Finally, activity is high in the hypothalamus and amygdala during dreaming. This explains for the emotional as well as motivational content for dreams.

As you can see this Neurocognitive theory explains why we dream in a lot more depth and it explains certain elements of dreams in more detail.

BIBLIOGRAPHY

Lee Parker (author), Darren Seath (author) Alexey Popov (author), *Oxford IB Diploma Programme: Psychology Course Companion,* 2nd edition, OUP Oxford, 2017

Alexey Popov, *IB Psychology Study Guide: Oxford IB Diploma Programme,* 2nd edition, OUP Oxford, 2018

https://www.thinkib.net/psychology/page/22420/localization-plasticity

First accessed on 15th March 2019

https://mrseplinibpsychologyclassblog.wordpress.com/2017/12/08/schachter-singer-1962

First accessed on 15th March 2019

Eysenck, M. W., & Keane, M. T. (2015). Cognitive psychology: A student's handbook. Psychology Press.

Gleitman, H., Gross, J., & Reisberg, D. (2011) Psychology (8th International Student Edition). London: W.W. Norton.

GET YOUR EXCLUSIVE FREE 8 BOOK PSYCHOLOGY BOXSET AND YOUR EMAIL PSYCHOLOGY COURSE HERE!

https://www.subscribepage.com/psychologyboxset

Thank you for reading.

I hoped you enjoyed it.

If you want a FREE book and keep up to date about new books and project. Then please sign up for my newsletter at www.connorwhiteley.net/

Have a great day.

CHECK OUT THE PSYCHOLOGY WORLD PODCAST FOR MORE PSYCHOLOGY INFORMATION!

AVAILABLE ON ALL MAJOR PODCAST APPS.

About the author:

Connor Whiteley is the author of over 30 books in the sci-fi fantasy, nonfiction psychology and books for writer's genre and he is a Human Branding Speaker and Consultant.

He is a passionate warhammer 40,000 reader, psychology student and author.

Who narrates his own audiobooks and he hosts The Psychology World Podcast.

All whilst studying Psychology at the University of Kent, England.

Also, he was a former Explorer Scout where he gave a speech to the Maltese President in August 2018 and he attended Prince Charles' 70th Birthday Party at Buckingham Palace in May 2018.

Plus, he is a self-confessed coffee lover!

Please follow me on:

Website: www.connorwhiteley.net

Twitter: @scifiwhiteley

Please leave on honest review as this helps with the discoverability of the book and I truly appreciate it.

Thank you for reading. I hope you've enjoyed.

All books in 'An Introductory Series':

BIOLOGICAL PSYCHOLOGY 3RD EDITION

COGNITIVE PSYCHOLOGY 2ND EDITION

SOCIAL PSYCHOLOGY- 3RD EDITION

ABNORMAL PSYCHOLOGY 3RD EDITION

PSYCHOLOGY OF RELATIONSHIPS- 3RD EDITION

DEVELOPMENTAL PSYCHOLOGY 3RD EDITION

HEALTH PSYCHOLOGY

RESEARCH IN PSYCHOLOGY

A GUIDE TO MENTAL HEALTH AND TREATMENT AROUND THE WORLD- A GLOBAL LOOK AT DEPRESSION

FORENSIC PSYCHOLOGY

CLINICAL PSYCHOLOGY

FORMULATION IN PSYCHOTHERAPY

Other books by Connor Whiteley:

THE ANGEL OF RETURN

THE ANGEL OF FREEDOM

GARRO: GALAXY'S END

GARRO: RISE OF THE ORDER

GARRO: END TIMES

GARRO: SHORT STORIES

GARRO: COLLECTION

GARRO: HERESY

GARRO: FAITHLESS

GARRO: DESTROYER OF WORLDS

GARRO: COLLECTIONS BOOK 4-6

GARRO: MISTRESS OF BLOOD

GARRO: BEACON OF HOPE

GARRO: END OF DAYS

WINTER'S COMING

WINTER'S HUNT

WINTER'S REVENGE

WINTER'S DISSENSION

Companion guides:

BIOLOGICAL PSYCHOLOGY 2ND EDITION WORKBOOK

COGNITIVE PSYCHOLOGY 2ND EDITION WORKBOOK

SOCIOCULTURAL PSYCHOLOGY 2ND EDITION WORKBOOK

ABNORMAL PSYCHOLOGY 2ND EDITION WORKBOOK

PSYCHOLOGY OF HUMAN RELATIONSHIPS 2ND EDITION WORKBOOK

HEALTH PSYCHOLOGY WORKBOOK

FORENSIC PSYCHOLOGY WORKBOOK

Audiobooks by Connor Whiteley:

BIOLOGICAL PSYCHOLOGY

COGNITIVE PSYCHOLOGY

SOCIOCULTURAL PSYCHOLOGY

ABNORMAL PSYCHOLOGY

PSYCHOLOGY OF HUMAN RELATIONSHIPS

HEALTH PSYCHOLOGY

DEVELOPMENTAL PSYCHOLOGY

RESEARCH IN PSYCHOLOGY

FORENSIC PSYCHOLOGY

GARRO: GALAXY'S END

GARRO: RISE OF THE ORDER

GARRO: SHORT STORIES

GARRO: END TIMES

GARRO: COLLECTION

GARRO: HERESY

GARRO: FAITHLESS

GARRO: DESTROYER OF WORLDS

GARRO: COLLECTION BOOKS 4-6

GARRO: COLLECTION BOOKS 1-6

Business books:

TIME MANAGEMENT: A GUIDE FOR
STUDENTS AND WORKERS

LEADERSHIP: WHAT MAKES A GOOD
LEADER? A GUIDE FOR STUDENTS AND
WORKERS.

BUSINESS SKILLS: HOW TO SURVIVE THE
BUSINESS WORLD? A GUIDE FOR
STUDENTS, EMPLOYEES AND EMPLOYERS.

BUSINESS COLLECTION

GET YOUR FREE BOOK AT:
WWW.CONNORWHITELEY.NET

CPSIA information can be obtained
at www.ICGtesting.com
Printed in the USA
LVHW051733080421
683894LV00022B/890

9 781914 081361